HELEN'S STORY

ROSEMARY FOX

HELEN'S STORY

JB

JOHN BLAKE

Published by John Blake Publishing Ltd,
3, Bramber Court, 2 Bramber Road,
London W14 9PB, England

www.blake.co.uk

First published in hardback in 2006

ISBN 1 84454 200 9

British Library Cataloguing-in-Publication Data:

A catalogue record for this book is available from the British Library.

Design by www.envydesign.co.uk

Printed in Great Britain by CPD (Wales) Ltd, Ebbw Vale

1 3 5 7 9 10 8 6 4 2

Papers used by John Blake Publishing are natural, recyclable products
made from wood grown in sustainable forests. The manufacturing processes
conform to the environmental regulations of the country of origin.

To Helen and our wonderful family David,
Suzanne and Rosanna

Acknowledgements

Heartfelt thanks to Jack Ashley, Lord Ashley of Stoke, without whom this project would not have developed as successfully as it did.

Contents

Foreword by Rt Hon Lord Ashley of Stoke, C.H.

J ust imagine that in 1962 you have been blessed with a happy, healthy baby daughter and that overnight she is transformed into one who could never be normal and who suffers permanent mental handicap and convulsions. Then, as you sought explanations and challenged the Government's refusal of compensation, you were warned that you were damaging the vaccine programme and told to keep quiet. How, in that deferential age, would any woman react?

Even in those unenlightened days, when women were expected to keep their place, Rosemary Fox refused to condone this lamentable ethos, defied convention and began a modest, reasonable but determined campaign for compensation. It eventually involved the Ombudsman, a Royal Commission, the European Commission on Human

Rights, Parliament and the Prime Minister. According to the Secretary of State for Health, it was 'one of the best examples I have experienced of a group of people with a cause that they know is right changing the course of events....Their campaign was almost a perfect example of how a voluntary organisation should do its job.' These comments, however, came after years of acrimonious exchanges with him in the House of Commons.

Despite the compliments at the end of the campaign, during it Rosemary had to endure bitter condemnation for arousing 'unnecessary' fears about the vaccination programme. Indeed, all who helped her were similarly attacked, notwithstanding the severe damage to some children, testified by doctors and eventually admitted by the Ministry of Health. Rosemary had to face procrastination at all levels of Government, as well as vituperative personal attacks. There were even attempts to take over her organisation and expel her.

The rollercoaster hazards of these efforts to seek justice are faithfully recorded in this meticulous account. It is an honest, disturbing but ultimately inspiring story which resulted in a complete reversal of Government policy – to the benefit of all vaccine damaged children.

Jack Ashley

Introduction

'And 'twere a cheaper way
Better it were a brother died at once
Than that a sister, by redeeming him,
Should die for ever.'
William Shakespeare,
Measure for Measure, Act II Scene iv

The full implications of this quotation first occurred to me as I sat with Professor Gordon Stewart at the Edinburgh Festival Production of *Measure for Measure* in 1976. I was visiting him to talk about the few children who had been adversely affected by vaccine damage, taking part as they did in the mass vaccination programmes which had protected the majority from the threat of illness from infectious disease. For a few of those vaccinated, however, far from being a blessing, those vaccinations turned out to be a curse that would destroy their lives.

I had gone to Glasgow at Professor Stewart's invitation to show him the details I had been collecting since 1974 about children who had suffered severe reactions to various vaccinations and were brain damaged as a result. Professor Stewart had been concerned about this issue for some time and was himself collecting similar data through his work as Professor of Immunology at Glasgow University.

Having seen a reference to Professor Stewart's work in the national press, I decided to see if I could find his telephone number and ring him. I was a bit nervous about doing it as, at that stage, I had little – if any – contact with University Professors and was not quite sure how he would react to a phone call from an unknown mother asking him about his research.

'I hope you don't mind me phoning you like this,' I started, 'but I saw your name in the *Telegraph* recently, along with a report about your work collecting details about vaccine damage. I'm running a campaign about this and wonder if I could ask you to look at some of the details I have collected?'

'I would be very pleased to help,' he said. 'But first I would want to look at the details.'

He went on to say that he would soon be in my area, Warwickshire, on his way back to Glasgow from a holiday and that he would call in to see me.

True to his word, he called in with his wife, Nina, and we spent some time going through the letters I had received from parents who were convinced that their children's disabilities had stemmed from vaccination. I realised that I need not have worried about contacting him. He was a kind, sympathetic man with an easy manner and was already aware from his own case files of the tragedy of vaccine damage. At the end of our chat, he and his wife kindly invited me to stay with them in Glasgow, where I spent some pleasant days finding out more about his work.

I went to Professor Stewart's office at the University to look through some of his files and he introduced me to his secretary, Margaret, who was to prove immensely helpful in our ongoing work on the analysis of parents' reports about their children. During my stay, I joined them at the Edinburgh Festival production and, among my records of that time, is the programme from the show which contains what I regarded as a very appropriate reference to vaccine damage: 'individual sacrifice for majority benefit'.

My contact with Professor Stewart was to remain constant for the next 20 years, during which time he carried out a major study into the reports given by parents of the damage to their children which they regarded as having resulted from vaccination. His work formed part of the 1977 studies set up by the Secretary of State for Social Services into reported reactions to whooping cough vaccination. For example, an advisory panel under the chairmanship of Professor Dudgeon, a member of the Joint Committee on Vaccination and Immunisation (JCVI) was set up to examine 50 cases of serious reactions to vaccination given by me to the Committee on Safety of Medicines (CSM)

There was also an advisory panel chaired by Professor T W Meade of the Medical Research Council, which was asked to provide an expert analysis by epidemiological methods of the cases reported to the CSM.

Many of the reports had been handed to the CSM by me at their request and many others had been collected by Professor Stewart himself. Details of the study were published in *Whooping Cough*, a report issued by the Department of Health and Social Security in May 1981.

The report from Professor Dudgeon's committee stated that, in some cases, the reaction was such that an association with immunization seemed possible. Professor Meade's panel found that the cases were unsatisfactory for epidemiological purposes, because of inadequate methods for the systemic detection of events following the use of vaccines. 'This should not be taken as meaning that pertussis vaccine damage does not occur' the report said.

Before 1974, there was very little discussion of vaccine damage. Although some health experts were concerned about the possibility of some children being damaged, it was a subject that was seldom mentioned publicly. The media generally followed the official line that the benefits of vaccination outweighed the disadvantages and that it would be highly irresponsible for anyone to publish anything which might turn parents away from vaccinations offered for the protection of their children's health.

Some indication of how successful this concern was can be seen from the fact that although there was disquiet in medical circles about serious illnesses being caused by smallpox vaccination in the early 1960s, and concern about a measles vaccine withdrawn in 1968 following reports of damage and death following its use, very little of this information reached the public. There were some brief references in 1968 to the fact that the whooping cough vaccine in use up until then had little effect on the disease but could be causing brain damage in a few children. Parents knew nothing of this, and continued to bring their children to clinics believing only that they were protecting them from whooping cough. Vaccine-damaged children had never been talked about and, to quote a doctor expressing some concern about them in 1973, children who were damaged were 'left to lie where they fall'.

It was in 1973 that I began to question the morality of the State's attitude, which allowed a few children to suffer the disadvantages of vaccination without offering any warning beforehand of possible risk, and with a seemingly casual acceptance by the Department of Health of the devastating consequences. I became aware of some of these background details having had Helen, my daughter, suffer a severe reaction to a polio vaccination in 1962. She had been injected with a Salk vaccine – so called after the scientist who developed it – and I was then left to deal with the consequences. I had had a perfectly healthy, normal child in 1962; in 1973, at the age of 11, Helen was assessed as having a mental age of about three, and suffered constant convulsions and the upsets and illnesses associated with them. I was also told that she would never live a normal life and would need constant care.

I became determined to find out what action I could take which, while not making her better, might secure an acknowledgement of the debt which was owed to her and others in her position.

In September 1973, following some local publicity about Helen and another vaccine-damaged girl, parents with similar stories to tell made contact. A meeting with some of these parents was arranged, at which a decision was taken to set up the Association of Parents of Vaccine Damaged Children with the aims of 'establishing the reality of vaccine damage' and 'investigating the role and responsibility of the Government in making provision for those who were damaged'.

The campaign which followed lasted 27 years.

Rosemary Fox, February 2006

1

A Life Less Ordinary

Helen is my second daughter and was born on 8 February 1962. At the time, my husband David and I lived in Devon with our two-and-a-half-year-old daughter Suzanne in the bungalow which was to be our home for another few years. When Suzanne was born in 1960, my mother had come from Ireland on a visit to see her and decided to stay on for a while and to help me look after the baby. After a month or so we agreed that she should stay with us on a more permanent basis. At 64 she was tired of her farming life and wanted a change. Since I missed my job and wanted to go back to work, the arrangement was ideal for both of us. She stayed on until December 1961, which enabled me to continue my job as Secretary to the Directors of an engineering company until shortly before Helen's birth. The company made turbine blades for aircraft and the Directors had been involved with jet engines since their first work with Frank Whittle, the famous inventor of the jet engine. As a secretary, my work was fascinating and I had contacts with all kinds of interesting people in the aircraft industry.

When my mother left in 1961, I missed her help but she had been starting to worry about her own home and the farm, which was being looked after by my brother and she wanted to take over the reins again. From then on until her death in 1977, she came back for occasional visits and we sometimes went over to see her.

David was an engineer working for a national heating engineering company. His work was interesting and well-paid, but when I stopped working we really felt the difference to our joint income.

Helen was a chubby, happy baby who progressed normally until she was seven months old, when she had her first polio vaccination. She slept well, fed well and was altogether a pleasure to look after. We spent our days joining in local playgroups, visiting the pleasant beaches that were close by, or simply going out shopping, with Helen in her pram and Suzanne sitting on a pram seat.

The Health Visitor who had previously visited Suzanne came to see Helen about her immunisations when she was 3 months old, advising the triple (whooping cough, diphtheria and anti-tetanus) which she was given. We were advised to give her the polio vaccination, which she had in September 1962 at 7 months old.

If my mother had still been with me things might have

been very different. The previous year, on hearing that we had been advised that Suzanne should be vaccinated against measles – a new vaccine according to the Health Visitor – my mother had said, 'What on earth do you want to do that for? Children get measles and, if they are properly looked after, they recover.'

In private she had said to me, 'For heaven's sake don't do it.'

I hadn't argued with her.

Thank God I had listened to her as, years later, I was to discover that the measles vaccine in question was 'on trial' at the time and was later withdrawn following reports of deaths in vaccinated children.

When it came to the polio vaccination, however, Mother wasn't there to advise.

At that time, the vaccine used was an injected Salk-type vaccine, a similar type to the American vaccine manufactured in this country by Burroughs Wellcome, both of which did not have the risk of leading to the disease, unlike the oral polio vaccine.

The day after the vaccination in September 1962, when I went to pick Helen up from her morning nap I found her pale and comatose. She had vomited over herself and her cot and, as I walked around with her in my arms, waiting for her to wake up, I was worried about what might have caused her sickness. I decided that if she took her midday bottle it would mean she was not too ill, and when she fed normally I stopped worrying. However, within a day, the vomiting became projectile, travelling at least 4 feet across the room from where she was sitting, which was so unusual that I phoned the doctor.

'Leave it for a few days,' he said, 'but if she continues to vomit like that, call me again.'

When he called a day or so later, he diagnosed pyloric stenosis, describing it as a condition in which the pyloric valve flips back the milk rather than allowing it to pass to the stomach. A simple operation would be needed, the doctor said, but first he prescribed some medicine which might cure the condition.

I had been told that my sister-in-law had suffered a similar condition when she had been about six weeks old and had had a minor operation which cured the vomiting, so although I wasn't too happy about a surgical procedure, I wasn't too worried about the vomiting, which stopped after the prescribed medicine had been finished.

Our bungalow was part of a development surrounded by other bungalows in which lived other young mothers and babies. Four or five of us got together each morning to form a playtime group for the children and to provide a coffee session for the grown-ups. Helen was eight months old and, with her sister Suzanne, joined in happily with the children's games. Watching her crawling around and playing, I noticed that she would occasionally stop still for a second or two and then burp. The pyloric valve, I thought, was not quite right and I made a note to keep watching her so that I could check with the doctor to make sure she did not need that operation after all.

Then, one day, when she was 12 months old and was

standing holding on to the window ledge, she turned and fell flat on the floor. I just thought she had lost her balance but a friend with whom I was having coffee at the time said very seriously, 'There is something wrong with her – go and see the doctor.'

Looking into Helen's face as I picked her up, I was reminded of a girl who had been a classmate of mine when I was about 12 years old, who used to stop and stare during lessons and was said by the teacher to be having fits. Strangely enough, that girl used to position herself next to me to hold my hand when she felt a seizure coming on, and now my heart stopped, as I realised that Helen was probably going through the same thing – she must have been suffering from minor epileptic attacks since she first became ill at eight months.

The doctor was concerned and helpful when I went to see him to explain my fears. He remembered my visit after the vaccination but, like a lot of other doctors at the time who had never heard of vaccine damage, he had not regarded it as significant. He arranged blood tests and stool tests, but all were clear. He then started coming to the house occasionally hoping to see Helen during a seizure but, of course, it was always five or ten minutes after he left that the seizure started.

By the age of 18 months, the seizures had become major convulsions from which Helen has never recovered, and it was then that the round of hospital visits to consultants and specialists began; doctors of all kinds tried to discover the underlying cause of her condition and then determine what, if anything, could be done to cure it.

Having a sick child was bad enough, but constant visits to clinics and specialists added greatly to the distress. Every visit held the promise of a diagnosis or of a treatment which would cure the condition, but they just became causes of extra upset. Waiting around to see the specialist, undressing and weighing a fractious child because nurses wanted details for their records, all in a crowded waiting room full of other upset children and weary mothers was a nightmare. Finally getting to the specialist's room and sitting while he asked umpteen questions about the medical history, the medication, the child's behaviour, and then ultimately being given little more than a further appointment in a few months' time was immensely disappointing. Yet back we went time after time for further appointments hoping for some breakthrough.

These visits to specialists continue to the present day, although they are not so focused now on finding a cure, but are still necessary to assess and treat the various conditions which are created by Helen's disability. Her anti-convulsant drugs need constant monitoring; her allergic reactions to various substances need classifying and treating; and the fractures she has suffered in falls during epileptic seizures have required surgery. She is very fortunate nowadays in that she is under the care of a concerned specialist who sees her regularly to check her medication and refers her for any special treatment she needs.

We went from specialist to specialist trying to find a

cure until, in the end, we realised there was no cure and that coping with the condition as positively and practically as possible was the best way forward. Yet we learned something from each specialist: Dr Haas, at the Children's Hospital in Exeter, was the first to see Helen at 18 months old, and told me pyloric stenosis couldn't happen at 7 months. The pyloric vomiting was, he said, a sign of brain disturbance. This revived all the concerns I had about Helen's sudden illness after the vaccination and the damage it caused, which I mentioned to every doctor and specialist I saw in the following years. All disputed that such a thing was possible: 'Vaccination is protection,' they said, and could not possibly be a source of damage.

The visit to Dr Haas coincided with the date on which I was due to give birth to my third baby but I was so anxious to get expert help for Helen that I went ahead with the meeting. I think I did warn him that I might have to leave in a hurry, and he was very considerate! As it turned out, the baby arrived three days later on 3rd August and was given my mother's name, Rosanna.

Helen next saw Dr Ounsted at the Park Hospital in Headington, Oxford, when she was five years old. He was carrying out a study into 'naturally occurring convulsions in childhood' which was part of the reason he was interested in her case. The hospital provided accommodation for visiting mothers with young families and I stayed there with Helen and my youngest daughter, Rosanna, for five weeks while the doctors carried out their tests. The possibility of brain surgery was discussed, but having been told by Dr Ounsted that Helen had the same chance of being cured, of suffering further damage or simply of there being no change, we dismissed the idea.

Helen was then referred to Dr Brian Bower, an Oxford specialist and, for the first time, there was a breakthrough in what up until then had been the mystery of Helen's change from a happy, healthy baby to a brain-damaged one. Dr Bower focused on my concerns about Helen's vaccination and subsequent illness. He was, I discovered, studying reactions to whooping cough vaccination and had published a paper, along with Dr PM Jeavons, in the *British Medical Journal* in 1960 about children admitted to Great Ormond Street suffering severe illnesses within 24 hours of inoculation.

At the time of Helen's injection and reaction, I knew very little about vaccination. I had previously worked as secretary to the directors of an engineering company and had heard the Technical Director complain from time to time about the injections he had before travelling abroad, some of which made him ill. I knew also that there had been publicity about the Salk polio vaccine in America and rumours of damage and deaths following its use, but when I asked my Health Visitor about this, she said not to worry, 'you know what the Americans are like'. In my ignorance, I agreed with her, feeling that Americans were probably not as carefully organised and cautious as the authorities in the UK were.

Again, it was years later when I discovered that at the time of Helen's vaccination in 1962 the Department of

Health had decided to stop using Salk Vaccine and were promoting a new Sabin live virus vaccine instead. Clearly it hadn't been available at Helen's clinic at the time and she had been given the Salk: what difference, if any, it might have made if the Sabin had been available we will never know but even that vaccine is known to give polio to a small percentage of children.

There was an interesting debate in the House of Lords in December 1982 about the rights of vaccine-damaged children which told some of the story of Salk vaccine. Lord Hailsham, then Lord Chancellor, speaking on behalf of the Conservative government and arguing against any special provision for those who were damaged, said,

'I will tell a very short anecdote if I may to illustrate why I say that.'[that vaccination is not a public policy]. He went on to say that 30 years previously he had been placed in the position of having to decide 'whether to import a thing called the Salk vaccine ... The argument for importing it was that there was only a very small quantity available of a British vaccine which was safe and therefore if I did not import it there would be a large number of children who would not have any vaccine at all ... The argument against importing it was that there had recently occurred a thing called the Cutter incident as a result of which in the United States ... a number of children had not only caught polio from the vaccine but had died from it or had suffered permanent injury.'

Having sought advice from the Medical Research Council about whether, in view of the Cutter incident, it was safer for a child to be vaccinated or not to be vaccinated, he was told that it is much safer to run the risk of vaccination than not to run the risk.

'Therefore I challenge the view which has been put forward – and accepted I think with too great a facility by nearly every speaker in this debate – that the mere fact that the Government are on the side of vaccination gives the disabled child who suffers from the vaccination a better chance than the child who suffers and who has not been vaccinated and as he is only 3 years old has no responsibility at all who has caught the disease and who suffers permanent disability from it.'

Dr Bower agreed to look into Helen's case and collected her vaccination and medical records. He then gave us his opinion that the polio vaccination at seven months old and the illness which followed were the probable causes of Helen's condition. I was concerned at first that 'probable' was not a very definite diagnosis, but Dr Bower explained that it meant that it was the nearest thing to certainty in cases like vaccine damage which could only be assessed after the event.

Driving home after the consultation with Dr Bower, my husband and I first talked of our relief at finally knowing for certain what had caused Helen's brain damage.

'Just imagine,' I said, 'after all these years wondering about Helen's vaccination, we now know we were right to blame it for Helen's condition'

We both went on to wonder if there was anything we could do about it and David said 'We have let seven years pass and I wonder if something could have been done earlier to help her.'

For years, I had wondered whether anything I had done had harmed my daughter, or whether simple things like the food she ate, or even silly things like the material in her clothes and shoes, could be causing reactions. It is surprising how one's mind can come up with all sorts of ridiculous explanations for a condition which has no name. Now I had a specialist supporting my theory, and my suspicions about the vaccination had been fully justified; I was not mad to consider the vaccination as being the cause of Helen's disabilities, and I could at last 'put a name' to her condition. Only then could I begin to get on with accepting her condition and making the best possible provision for my daughter's future security and happiness.

My initial relief soon turned to anger at the realisation that her vaccination had changed her from a healthy to a disabled child. I had taken a healthy child to a clinic on the advice of a Health Visitor acting for a Health Authority carrying out the wishes of a Government Health Department, having been told that it was to protect Helen's health but without any warning of any possible risk. What I had not been told and did not fully realise was that Helen was just a statistic in the immunisation process – one child among thousands who had to be vaccinated to meet the Health Authorities' programme of wiping out disease and preventing its return, the success of which depended on getting the largest possible number of children vaccinated. It seemed to me that, somewhere along the line, the need to protect the rights of any child who might be injured in this way had been overlooked, so I decided for Helen's sake and for the sake of any others in her position to start an investigation, which turned into a campaign.

Today, Helen is 43 years old. For the past ten years she has been happily settled in a small residential home with a high level of caring and qualified staff. She has constant family contact and home visits. The decision to place her in the home was another heartbreak for Helen's father and me, but knowing that we would most probably die before her, we had to make sure that she was happily settled in another 'home' while we were still alive and able to satisfy ourselves that she was happy and well cared for. Some parents cannot cope with arranging residential care for their children and hope that brothers and sisters will eventually take over the care. There are others like us who feel that care is best placed in the hands of a statutory authority which ensures long-term continuity.

Helen is a happy, affectionate young woman and, although she does not speak, she understands what is said to her. She is one of five residents in her care home and has a settled routine. They take her shopping, walking and on interesting day trips. An aromatherapist goes to see her once a week and there are outings to sensory rooms which she finds relaxing.

Twice a week, she goes to a special day centre run by social services. The brilliant staff organise many activities such as swimming and riding. Recently they told me they were taking her ice skating – which was really surprising! They explained that they took the wheelchairs on the rink and the carers skated around with them. I am told Helen loves it, as do the others.

Without all her very caring helpers, she would not be able to do any of these things and I am constantly reminded of how much we, her parents, and Helen herself, owe to the wonderful people who are prepared to take on the care of disabled people.

She continues to take anti-convulsant medication which has reduced the number of her severe seizures, but it is clear that both the medication and the seizures have had a disastrous effect on any chance she may have had to develop normally. She has a lovely face with a completely normal expression and it is difficult sometimes for others to understand that she is brain damaged. She cannot look after herself; left alone in a house full of food, she would not know how to feed herself or ask for help.

The greatest worry to all parents of the disabled is what will happen to their children after they have died. At least we know that Helen is happy in her home, that she has caring staff to look after and love her and that she has two sisters who will make sure she continues to be well and happy.

2

Who Knew What?

Thinking about how to start a campaign, I decided that the first requirement was intelligent publicity, supported by some official reports on the arguments in question. In 1973, however, it was very difficult to get any publicity started about vaccination as the media followed the official view that any criticism of vaccinations or vaccination policy would be highly irresponsible. Vaccination was, the Department of Health said, one of the greatest success stories in the history of medicine in modern times. The benefits greatly exceeded the disadvantages, the Department added, listing the benefits as freedom from disease for all who were vaccinated and the resultant significant savings in medical costs which infectious diseases caused. The disadvantages were never mentioned.

Looking for medical arguments which would support any campaign, I found a Public Health Laboratory Service report in the *British Medical Journal* of 3 February 1973, which reported that the whooping cough vaccine in use for five or six years before 1968 was not very effective, following which the potency of the vaccine was increased.

Reading further, I found copy of a presentation by the late Professor George Dick to an International Symposium on Combined Vaccines in 1967, which referred to his report on reactions to the pertussis (whooping cough) element of the triple vaccine (combining diphtheria, tetanus and whooping cough), in which he said that, based on reports from two cities in the UK, up to 80 cases of brain damage could occur each year from its use. Showing a great deal of concern for children in vaccination programmes, he was worried about the suggestion that the strength of the vaccine should be doubled and he argued that, if this was done, then children should not be offered the vaccine until they were six months old, instead of three months according to the policy at the time.

Going back even further, I found the *British Medical Journal* report of July 5 1958, in which Dr JM Berg of the Fountain Hospital, London, not only discussed what he called the seventh case of brain damage from whooping cough vaccination in Great Britain, but also referred to an analysis of many similar cases reported in other countries.

For instance, there was a report by Byers and Moll in

1948 citing 15 infants from 5 to 18 months old, none of whom had suffered previous convulsions, all of whom suffered reactions after vaccination, within 20 minutes or 72 hours. Two infants died from pneumonia, five suffered hemiplegia (paralysis of one side of the body), two became decebrate (damage to the brain), five suffered mental retardation and only one recovered.

I also discovered many other reports published between 1949 and 1965, some of which had been sent directly to the Ministry of Health; many are listed in a reference section at the end of this book. These reports were published in the medical press but received no national publicity which could have alerted parents to possible danger. Neither, it appears, did the reports cause concern to the Department of Health officials whose strong promotion of whooping cough vaccination in the UK began around 1957. A total of 187 cases of severe reaction to whooping cough vaccination was eventually built up.

I also found reports about damage following the use of Salk polio vaccine in America and following measles vaccine when it was first introduced in the UK in 1968.

I had never heard of any of these reports and, having started out more or less tentatively suggesting that I was sure vaccination had injured my daughter, I found them amazing and upsetting. They strengthened my resolve to raise the whole issue of vaccine damage publicly in the interests of those who had suffered .

I had mentioned all of this to Dr Harris, Helen's doctor at the time and although, like many other doctors in the

17

early 1970s, he knew little about vaccine damage, he was helpful and encouraging, but had little more to offer.

Then, one morning, I was out and about in my local area when I ran into Dr Harris again. He seemed glad to have the opportunity to stop and chat, and it became clear that he wanted to give me an article of some sort. Glancing at it, I realised that it related to Helen's condition, and that it would confirm that I was not alone. Indeed, it also confirmed that the authorities elsewhere in Europe had already started to take action on vaccination-related conditions, and that perhaps there was now some official acknowledgement that governmental bodies had to take some responsibility for the outcome of their immunisation programmes.

When I got a chance to read the article in detail, I was astonished. What I had in my hands was a report of an International Symposium on Vaccination against Communicable Diseases held in Monaco that year, 1973, in which not only was vaccine damage discusssed in detail, but one section was devoted to a discussion by a German health official on 'compensation for injuries possibly related to immunisation'. The German Government, I discovered, had introduced a compensation scheme for injuries relating to immunisation as far back as 1962, which was later amended when more experience of the kinds of injuries and the circumstances in which they had occurred was available. Under the German scheme, medical and other costs were covered by regular payments and there was also a pension scheme to cover any disability where earning capacity was impaired.

I was utterly amazed – I had spent ten years worrying about Helen's condition and wondering about the cause of it, but had never seen or heard of any of the publicity which would have made these details public knowledge. I had never met anyone who knew about vaccine damage and couldn't understand how I could have missed any reference to what appeared to be a closely guarded secret.

If anything was needed to convince me that I had a right to say publicly that children in this country had been vaccine damaged and that the Government had a responsibility to make special provision for them, this article was it. I was now convinced that I had valid grounds for starting a campaign for compensation for my daughter and for anyone else injured in the same way. I was well aware that I would be criticised by sections of the medical profession and that the media might be reluctant to get involved. Vaccination had always been the 'sacred cow' of medicine, and any questions raised about any aspect of it were not welcomed. Despite my reservations, though, and the inevitable criticism that would come my way, I felt I owed it to my daughter and all those current and future victims to let others know what I knew, and so bring the Government to account and offer others the freedom to make informed choices about their children's lives.

3

The Association

Helen was the only vaccine-damaged child I knew at the time, and I wondered how I might track down any of the children mentioned in the published reports, in order to meet their parents and hear their stories.

At around that time, a party was arranged by the manager of the playgroup for disabled children which Helen attended and, while sitting watching the children enjoying themselves, I saw another young girl whose behaviour seemed to be very similar to Helen's. She, too, looked completely normal, but in a roomful of quiet children she was running around in circles just like Helen. Her name was Joanne Lennon and when I asked her mother, Rene, what had been the cause of her disability, I was amazed when she said 'polio vaccination'. It then occurred to me that I had details of at least two cases as a starting point in my search for others.

The easiest way to contact other affected families was to have a story published in the press, but knowing that this might not be easy, because of the fear of the public media being branded irresponsible, I thought our local newspaper might be a good place to start, if, indeed, they were prepared to write the story.

Celia Hall, now the medical editor of the *Telegraph*, was the Health Correspondent for the *Birmingham Post* at the time and I phoned her to discuss the possibility of an article about the two girls. She agreed to meet Joanne's mother and myself and, after a long talk about the background to the girls' condition, agreed to cover the story. At the time, I think she, too, was conscious of the criticism it might attract from the medical profession but, as the tattered yellow memo slip in my file which she brought with her shows, she had done her homework. Celia had first checked to see if there were any expert references to reactions to vaccination, and had brought with her what was listed as 'Dr Millar's Patent Preventative Reading List'. In this was listed a series of references to conditions linked to the aftermath of various vaccines, all of which confirmed that vaccine damage was a reality and something which would bear discussion. Again, it was clear that details of damage following vaccination had been available for many years and what was surprising was that the public had never been informed. Her detailed article about Helen and

Joanne appeared in the *Birmingham Post* on 26 June 1973.

Under a large headline reading, WHOSE BURDEN? there were photographs of Helen and Joanne and details of the reactions which had caused their damage. The article stated:

'It said on Helen Fox's clinic card Protect YOUR child by vaccination ... For Helen the irony of that sound advice is bitter.'

It went on to describe the development of Helen's convulsions, the numerous visits to doctors and specialists. The article told the story of her life up to 1973 when it became clear that, despite suggestions from some doctors that she might not live beyond the age of 8; and despite suggestions from a Health Visitor to 'send her away as she will ruin your life and that of your other children', Helen had settled down and was attending a special school in Stratford upon Avon.

'She is now obedient but she does like running away,' stated the article. 'Her father is now building the garden wall a foot higher to stop her getting out because when she runs, she's off!'

'"Joanne was an adorable baby,"' the article said, quoting her mother Rene.

At 13 months, Joanne had a polio vaccination and three days later was critically ill, had a violent convulsion and was rushed into hospital. She stayed there for six weeks suffering constant convulsions and Rene was told her baby would be a degenerate. When the convulsions stopped Joanne slept for hours and one day when Rene went to see her she thought Joanne looked so normal sleeping that she was filled with hope until Joanne opened her eyes and was, 'just a babbling child, not seeing or hearing.' She was eight when the article was written and her mother described her then as 'a pretty little girl. Most of her problems can be solved with a kiss.'

Referring to an article in the *British Medical Journal* which was arguing for a compensation scheme for vaccine damage, Celia Hall added that we now wanted to form a society so that from a position of strength we could put pressure on the Government for a compensation scheme.

Helen was then eleven years old. Seeing the story in print brought home to me again the tragedy which had resulted from my consent to vaccination without any knowledge of risk. It also strengthened my resolve to do something positive about it.

Rene and I had agreed that I would deal with the secretarial side and the publicity, while she would provide backup and moral support and together we would set up meetings with other parents.

The Guardian followed the *Birmingham Post*'s lead with another detailed article about the girls and my proposed campaign for them and, as a result of these two articles, I received 28 letters from parents with a similar story to tell. A total of 28 cases was, I thought then, quite a considerable number, but little did I know of the hundreds of letters which were to pour in in the coming months.

It was during the interview for the *Birmingham Post* that

a name for the fledgling campaign group was decided on
– The Association of Parents of Vaccine Damaged
Children. It is undeniably a long title that doesn't lend
itself to an interesting abbreviation, and there were
criticisms of it from time to time from the media. The
families involved, however, came to know it as 'The
Association', which continues to be its informal title to
the present day.

Reading through the first batch of letters was incredibly
upsetting. We were used to coping with our own tragedies
but, thinking they were fairly unique, it was a shock to
find how many other families were suffering as well. Most
wrote about convulsions; some had children who were
partially paralysed. I was aware that the letters were
mostly from local, very literate families and it was
obvious that I needed a popular newspaper to contact
parents nationally. At that point, Jean Carr of the *Sunday
Mirror* phoned to say that she was interested in the story
and wanted details for an article. The article appeared one
Sunday in August 1973.

A week went by and then, on the following Monday
morning, the telephone rang very early. It was Jean Carr
asking me to go down to the *Mirror* offices to help to
answer the hundreds of phone calls and enquiries which
had poured into the *Mirror* since my article had appeared.
Parents from all over the country were phoning to tell
their stories and nearly all said they thought they were the
only ones to whom this had happened. Listening to what
they had to say, and later reading their letters, I needed no

further convincing that what I was about to embark on was fully justified. Far from being a 'one in a million chance', as the Department of Health liked to call the possibility of damage from vaccination, what I and many other parents had thought of as something which had unfortunately happened to our child alone had been a far more common occurrence. By the end of 1973, I had received around 280 letters from parents. Nearly all said 'I thought I was the only one' and 'I have been a voice crying in the wilderness because no one would listen when I said vaccination caused the damage'.

The vaccinations mentioned covered all of those in routine use at the time – measles, smallpox, oral and injected polio vaccine, rubella (given at school), BCG, and the triple of diphtheria, tetanus and whooping cough. Three out of every four letters indicated the cause as being the triple, and most blamed the whooping cough part of the triple, which was the reason why whooping cough vaccination became the most talked about during the campaign.

At that stage, with a list of 280 families anxious to take part in the Association's campaign, I selected a number of replies from parents living in Warwickshire and asked them if they would like to come to a meeting in Birmingham to talk about starting a campaign for our children. About 12 people agreed and one was able to arrange the use of a small church hall.

I recall it was a pleasant summer evening and I picked up Rene on the way to Birmingham and we talked excitedly about what looked like a promising start to our fight for our daughters.

David had to stay at home to look after the rest of the family as did Joanne's father. While it was very easy for families with 'normal' children to arrange babysitters or leave their children with strangers, this was never the case for those of us with children who needed special care. Not only would we be worried about whether they would be looked after properly but it was not easy to find people prepared to look after them. It is only in recent years that a greater awareness of disability has created a greater willingness on the part of the public generally to accept disabled people as being no different from anyone else. In the seventies, however, this was not the case so mothers and fathers had to split the babysitting between them.

Having arrived at the hall and introduced ourselves to the other parents, we spent some time telling each other our stories and I explained how I wanted to go about setting up a campaign group. We talked about how difficult it was to get doctors and professionals to accept that vaccine damage was real. The most common statement from parents writing to us was, 'I was a voice crying in the wilderness' i.e. no one would take what they were saying seriously. So the first thing we had to do was to collect and publish reports from experts who knew what we were talking about. We then had to go to the Government and tell them that if some European countries – such as Denmark, Germany, Hungary, Norway and Japan – were taking responsibility for the damage created and paying compensation to the sufferers, there should be a similar scheme for our children.

Our aims were set out as:

1. To establish the reality of vaccine damage
2. To seek some kind of insurance of the scheme in order to protect the rights of those who were damaged

As a novice group our aims were not clearly worded and were later to be corrected by Barbara Castle, who pointed out that insurance was for future events and would not cover for any past events. What we were really saying was that we wanted to prove that our children were vaccine damaged and we wanted the State to make special provision for them.

It was decided that parents would be asked to contribute £2 each to fund the work that would be necessary but it was also decided that we would not be a very formal group with detailed rules and regulations. It was agreed that I would act as Honorary Secretary, calling on others in the group for help as necessary, and also that we did not want to get involved in the minutiae of rules about meetings, quorums, members' voting rights and all the other aspects of formal constitutions. As a campaign group, we would not qualify for charity status and, since all our efforts would be concentrated on the work involved, we would not have any care/welfare/advice role which might divert our efforts.

Our one concession to formality was the decision to have account details audited annually to ensure there could never be any suggestion that collected funds were incorrectly handled, and one parent whose daughter had reacted to a measles vaccination, but had fortunately recovered, offered her help as Treasurer. All monies went to her and were audited and we stuck strictly to our auditor's advice that we should never seek or accept large sums from external organisations or raise more than the amount needed to cover postage, phone calls and travel expenses.

The decision taken not to have a formal constitution proved to be very important years later when some parents formed a splinter group and wanted to take over the running of the Association and the campaign, expecting to see a constitution with rules which would enable them to do so. Stories abound of groups in which a few members become dissatisfied, criticise the founders and go over their heads to the other members seeking their votes for a change in the constitution which would allow new leaders to be appointed. Where this succeeds, it must be a very bitter blow for anyone who has worked hard to get a project off the ground and running successfully, only to be dismissed at the whim of a few dissatisfied people. Although such a possibility never occurred to me when making the original informal arrangements for our group, I was very glad much later on that our arrangements made it impossible.

Following our Birmingham meeting – and with nearly 300 reports from parents all over the country – I wrote to ask if any parent would like to act as an Area Secretary to keep in touch with parents in their region. Part of their job would be to pass on information quickly and to encourage the parents in their area to keep in touch with their Members of Parliament. I thought that this arrangement would work much better than an elected committee governed by rules and regulations. 13 parents from various parts of the country agreed. This arrangement worked well until the first breakthrough in 1979 when the Vaccine Damage Payment Act was passed.

Scotland already had its own campaign figurehead in Helen Scott, whose son had been damaged by smallpox vaccination and she had been fighting for him. Her case load was to increase greatly when news of our campaign spread and Scottish parents wrote with their stories. Helen continued to lead the campaign with parents in Scotland and was a valuable source of information and help over the years. In Northern Ireland, the parent of another victim of smallpox vaccination provided a contact for parents there which meant that the campaign now covered the whole of the UK.

These informal arrangements not only proved to be highly effective but also removed the possibility of any friction arising from arguments or differences of opinion among members of an elected committee. It was to be 25 years later that such a committee was formed and almost immediately led to arguments and upsets.

4

Building the Case

By early 1974, we had well organised, informal arrangements covering nearly 300 families with a number of dedicated parents helping to keep the campaign alive in their areas. Local meetings were organised, the press was kept informed and Members of Parliament were approached for their support. Among some of the activities organised to publicise the campaign was the printing of a car sticker which read 'VACCINE DAMAGED CHILDREN NEED JUSTICE' and this appeared on cars all over the country.

Eight months previously I had been sitting wondering if I could manage to carry the workload I knew would be involved in the campaign I wanted to start. Now there were numerous families ready to help and a widespread organisation to rely on. Helen was twelve and healthy

31

apart from her convulsions. I had a supportive family and was beginning also to make contact with organisations that cared for disabled children and provided occasional holidays and some overnight care.

I could now devote time to raising the issues with the Government and for this the first essential was to ensure that the facts and figures to be presented were clear and unambiguous. With reports from nearly 300 families to bring together, a detailed analysis of the information was a first priority.

It is inevitable when stories of any particular illnesses or accidents – especially those affecting children – appear in the press, that large numbers of people will identify with the details given and say that is what happened to them. In order to be sure that I was presenting clear details of vaccine-damaged children, rather than a collection of details of disabled children, I designed a simple questionnaire form which parents were asked to fill in. This asked for the child's name and date of birth, the date and type of vaccination, details of the reaction which followed vaccination and a note of the interval between vaccination and reaction. Parents were also asked to say if they had reported the reaction to their clinic or doctor and what the response was to any such report. I was not qualified to determine the child's state of health prior to the vaccination, but I knew that when the questionnaires came to be examined, as I was confident they would be, the necessary medical histories would be sought by examining specialists.

This specific detail is vital for anyone making a claim about vaccine damage today. A surprising number of claimants seem to think that all that is required is a letter or telephone call to the Vaccine Damage Payment Unit, which was set up in 1978 to check claims, saying that they or their children were vaccine damaged and thinking that the Payment Unit will do the rest. Any claim needs as much supporting evidence as possible and the claimant is the best person to look for it and send it on for checking.

When I met Professor Stewart during my trip to Glasgow in 1976, he looked at the questionnaires and considered that they would give a satisfactory first history. When he was later a member of the team which examined cases for the Department of Health, he extended the questionnaire to include additional medical details, but I was pleased to note that the basics of my simple questionnaire remained a constant part of future medical studies.

One thing which became immediately obvious from the questionnaires was that three out of every four families blamed the triple vaccination – the combined diphtheria, tetanus and whooping cough vaccines. There had not been any adverse publicity about either of the first two components and the blame for the damage was laid at the door of the whooping cough vaccine which had been the subject of criticism from time to time. Having started off with the knowledge only of the effects of polio vaccination, it was necessary to investigate whooping cough vaccine as a possible cause of most of the cases of damage on my files.

It was at about this time that I read of the research by Dr John Wilson, Consultant Neurologist at Great Ormond Street Hospital for Sick Children. Dr Wilson had examined the case histories of a number of children suffering severe illnesses within 24 hours of vaccination and published a report on the subject.

Following my initial contact with Professor Stewart and now having a bit more confidence in talking about vaccine damage, I decided to phone Dr Wilson to talk about the details I had collected. It isn't easy for laymen to venture into highly professional expert areas and, until I had met Dr Wilson, I wasn't sure what my reception would be. I needn't have worried. Dr Wilson agreed to meet me at Great Ormond Street Hospital. He was pleasant and helpful and took time out from his busy day to look at my file. He told me which of the cases could be considered as 'probable' and which were 'possible' and by the time I left him I knew a great deal more about how to sort out all the details sent to me by parents.

Before I left he said, 'You have to be aware that you will probably be criticised by some of my medical colleagues for what they will see as raising doubts about vaccination.' I couldn't help but wonder if he had suffered criticism following his report.

Following Dr Wilson's advice on possible and probable cases, I then divided the families and their letters into two groups, one to which I could offer membership of the

Association as being probable cases. The other group I could only offer to ensure that, when the time came, their details would be passed on to the Government. I did this knowing there would be critics who would say that this was just a scare campaign, without any basis for claiming damage, and I had to ensure that the details would stand up to scrutiny. Indeed, it was not long before the Chairman of the Joint Committee on Vaccination and Immunisation which advises the Government and promotes vaccination publicly said my files were 'just a collection of cases seeking compensation for disabled children'.

Dr Wilson's help at the time was invaluable and gave me the confidence I needed to present my case, based on all the details I had collected.

Over the years, Dr Wilson continued to be a source of help and advice to the Association, accompanying us to meetings where medical matters were likely to be discussed. For example, he helped with the evidence to the Royal Commission on Civil Liability and Compensation for Personal Injury (the Pearson Commission) which recommended 'strict liability' for vaccine damage and he accompanied us to meetings with the Department of Health when they wanted to tell us about their programme of MMR vaccination. Without the help, support and dedication of professionals and experts like Dr Wilson, our campaign might never have got off the ground, and would certainly have floundered when others sought to discredit us.

5

Getting Into Parliament

It was in August 1973 when the question of raising the issue in the House of Commons came up. I knew little about how campaigns worked and, apart from voting for our local Member of Parliament at election times, I knew less about how Members of Parliament worked. Clearly, we needed a strong advocate in Parliament to raise the question of vaccine damage and pursue the Government on the question of making special provision for those who had suffered.

At the time, a local group of the charity Action for the Crippled Child had been set up in Stratford and I went along to some of the evening meetings. It was at one of these meetings, while I was talking about my own child and my hope of running a campaign in Parliament, that one of the Committee members mentioned Jack Ashley.

Due to his constant work for disabled children he was well known to the charity executives.

I had, of course, heard of Jack Ashley MP, who suffered deafness following an operation which destroyed his promising career, or so it was said at the time. There are many who have since said that far from ruining his life, his disability enabled him and left him free to devote all his energies to helping others, and the list of those he has helped over the years is endless. This is perhaps a selfish way of looking at it as I am sure that Jack himself had his own dreams of what he wanted to do and what he could achieve in many other important fields. I wrote to him and he agreed to meet me, asking me to bring along a brief outline of what I was proposing.

I told Celia Hall about the impending meeting and on the day of the meeting in The Birmingham Post there was an article reading, 'Today Rosemary Fox goes to Parliament with a file of stories about vaccine damaged children which she hopes will be the start of a campaign for State provision for them'

I bought a new coat and had my hair done and hoped that I would appear competent and intelligent. The train would take me to Paddington from where I would take the tube to Westminster and, I thought, get to the meeting in good time. But it was not to be so simple. The train stopped for nearly half an hour on the approach to Paddington and I was aware of each minute ticking by, wondering if I would ever get to the meeting. To save whatever time I could I took a taxi from Paddington to the House of Commons where the meeting was to take place. Then there was a further delay while I had to check in and send my briefcase through the security barrier. By this time I was a nervous wreck!

'Please,' I said to the attendant, 'I am very late for a meeting. Could you show me quickly where the committee room is?'

The staff were very helpful and I finally arrived at the meeting. Sitting around a table were Jack Ashley and his wife, Pauline, with Professor Dick, Duncan Guthrie, Chairman of Action for the Crippled Child, and another colleague.

I was afraid that I wouldn't make a very good impression because of my late arrival I had kept everyone waiting and there was no way I could have let them know what had happened. Today, I would have a mobile phone and the problem would not arise but this was 1973. As well as I could, speaking from conviction and from the data I had accumulated, I told them why I believed that some children had been damaged by vaccination and why the State had a responsibility to make special provision for them.

To begin with, I was nervous about this as I wanted to make my case directly to Jack Ashley, but I was not sure how I would be able to do this if he could not hear what I was saying. I had been told that he would able to lip read, but would I be able to form my words clearly enough for him to understand? I need not of course have worried because Pauline, Jack's wife, was there to make sure that he could understand everything that was said either by repeating it clearly or by writing it down. I came to know Pauline well over the years and never ceased to admire her constant cheerfulness and patience when helping people to speak to Jack. I hoped that, over time, I would be able to speak so that Jack could easily read my lips, but I wasn't always successful and, once, to cover up my shortcomings, I told him that he was probably having difficulty understanding me because 'I am speaking with an Irish accent!' Pauline's helpful presence was a great help to me and, I am sure, to countless others.

Indeed, Pauline's involvement was not confined to liaising with those seeking Jack's help. She was an active campaigner in her own right and played an important role in many of the good causes devoted to helping those who needed advice and support. Jack himself said that she was often more passionately involved in the campaigns than he was and that she provided invaluable ideas, suggestions and research for all the issues he pursued publicly, which included Thalidomide, domestic violence, bullied soldiers, drug damage, rape victims and others.

This first meeting was pleasant and informative, with Professor Dick confirming that there was a case to answer and, after the meeting, Jack Ashley asked me to provide him with facts and figures to enable him to raise the matter in Parliament. Professor Dick provided me with references to the expert research on whooping cough vaccination in particular and, afterwards, he continued to give me advice and guidance in the preparation of our campaign material. He was always concerned that our campaign should be as responsible and non-controversial as possible and one of his particular requests was that we should never refer to our children as victims.

Professor Dick was a member of the Joint Committee on Vaccination and Immunisation, which was set up to advise the Department of Health on vaccination. He had his own reservations about the whooping cough vaccine and had published reports on its possible side effects. At the time, he was also concerned about the side effects of smallpox vaccination and argued for its withdrawal.

I was unable to agree with the suggestion made by Duncan Guthrie that the campaign should cover all disabled children, not just those who were vaccine damaged. Like others, he thought that the more money spent on special cases, the less would be available for charities. We were a very small, new group without the staff, office facilities or funding which would have enabled us to carry out the kind of campaign he had in mind and which was already being carried out by charities like Action for the Crippled Child. I did not see our campaign as detracting from the work of others and I was completely convinced, and always have been since, that healthy children who became disabled by the action of the State in the interests of community health merited very special consideration, far above what the State was likely to provide for disabled children generally.

This has always been a very difficult argument to maintain, because to the parent of a child who is born disabled, or becomes disabled by illness or accident, there is no difference. Disability is disability, however it occurs, and arguing special cases can sound selfish. My argument however, which I still maintain, is that when higher levels of provision are achieved for special cases like ours, comparisons are created which can help to improve provision for all. When the meeting finished Jack Ashley promised that he would ask for a Parliamentary Debate on the subject.

When I went to that November meeting, I had received details from 28 families about their vaccine-damaged children. By the time Jack Ashley had applied for and been given a date for what was the first ever Parliamentary Debate about vaccine damage, the numbers had risen to nearly 300. There was great excitement among the families when I told them that there was to be a debate in the House of Commons on 31 January 1974, at which Jack would put forward the case on behalf of our children who had been damaged by vaccinations of various kinds, and ask the Government to make special provision to enable us to care for them properly.

I went down to hear the debate. It was my first proper visit to the House of Commons.

Having given my name and the reason for my visit, quoting Jack Ashley as my reference, I was able to look around the lobby and saw all the statues of famous politicians and look at the impressive floors and ceilings.

Sitting on a side seat, I watched Members of Parliament

passing in and out of the Chamber, meeting constituents or walking briskly with briefcases on urgent business. Standing near one long corridor I had to move to one side to let Ian Paisley, dressed in black, walk past – but I didn't dare say hello.

As the debate was an evening or adjournment debate I had plenty of time to look around and be impressed by all the activity. Jack, who had been in the House during the day, came to the lobby with Professor Dick late in the afternoon and told me the BBC wanted to do an interview with us about the debate. Further excitement!

I was taken to a BBC studio nearby and escorted into a long, brightly lit room where a young girl was ready with make up and lipstick to paint me. I told her that I didn't really like make up and asked her why it was necessary but she said it was because of the very bright studio lights and without it I would look like a ghost. Fortunately I wasn't aware until much later that I looked fairly unusual for me, with rosy cheeks, bright lipstick and blue eyes.

It was a fairly brief interview. Jack outlined the case for compensating children damaged by vaccination while Professor Dick confirmed from his own research that some children had been – and were being – damaged by whooping cough vaccination in particular although he referred to the severe effects of the smallpox vaccination as well. I was asked what kind of cases I had collected and how many parents had joined the Association which was set up to campaign. It was clear that the media regarded the subject as very new and perhaps controversial.

Afterwards, Jack took myself and Professor Dick for tea in the House of Commons Visitors' Dining Room and after that excitement I went up to the Visitor's, or Strangers', Gallery to hear the Debate. Looking down onto the floor of the House I could see a number of Members of Parliament; some were waiting to participate in Jack's debate about vaccine damaged children and some were waiting for a later debate on historic buildings. Sitting in the gallery I was excited and pleased to think that my dream of getting recognition and recompense for my daughter and others who had suffered in the same way was about to be fulfilled.

It was 8.34 pm when the debate was called.

'The purpose of this debate is to tear aside the veil of obscurity which has shrouded the fate of thousands of children, to suggest urgent action aimed at reducing the number of future tragedies and to offer proposals to compensate those who are severely damaged,' Jack started. 'An eminent virologist of international repute has spoken of a "conspiracy of silence" about reactions to a vaccine and warned that authorities "try to muzzle critics" The suffering of vaccine damaged children and their families is appalling.'

He went on to tell the stories of some of the damage that had been inflicted. 'Carolyn cannot walk, talk or help herself in any way … and at 13 has no mental age at all'

A ten-year-old boy 'has had fits daily ever since his injection, has as many as 12 fits a day … has three drugs three times a day and has to continually wear a crash helmet to avoid injury to himself.'

During the debate, and raising the question of how many cases of adverse reaction were there, Jack quoted the reply he had received from the Secretary of State for Health and Social Services two days previously, to a written question on the subject, to which the answer given was, 'the majority of adverse reactions are not reported.'

This was, Jack said, 'a serious admission of gross neglect,' and he said that this daunting human cost can be reduced by resolute Government action and the co-operation of the medical profession. He urged that the Government should do much more to reduce the risks and should also set up a state compensation scheme to underwrite the immunisation programme.

It was a passionate speech which highlighted all the flaws and failings in the promotion of the immunisation programme which had led to a situation where children had been and were being damaged without, it seemed, causing any concern to the health officials responsible for immunisation.

I sat on the edge of my seat, shaking with nerves and excitement, waiting to hear the response from the Conservative Under-Secretary of State for Health and Social Security, Michael Alison. Once he had risen to his feet, he spent a very long time outlining the history of immunisation, referring to the Joint Committee on Vaccination and Immunisation as the body set up to advise the Health Ministers about vaccination programmes and to review the vaccines in use. He referred to the withdrawal of smallpox vaccination in

1971 as 'a historic decision' taken by the Joint Committee, because the vaccine had proved so effective in dealing with the disease that it was no longer required. What he did not say was that statistics gathered by the Health Department for years showed that smallpox vaccine was causing a significant number of serious reactions and that at least one reason for its withdrawal was serious concern by Professor Dick, a member of the Joint Committee, that the vaccine was creating more damage than was ever likely to occur from smallpox at the time.

'No immunising procedure is entirely free from risk,' Mr Alison stated, adding that precise estimates of the degree of risk were difficult to make. He then made the surprising statement that the fact that there were risks was generally known but that 'it is a moot point how far it is desirable to do more to warn individuals or parents about possible risks when these are exceedingly remote.' This brought Jack Ashley to his feet to ask if the Minister was suggesting that it was a deliberate act of Government policy to hide the truth, but Mr Alison passed the responsibility for discussing this to doctors.

He finally arrived at the question of compensation and said it was the Government's view that the granting of compensation in these cases was not 'appropriate or feasible'. It was the use of the word 'appropriate' that made me so angry; it indicated such a degree of insensitivity and lack of understanding that I found it hard to restrain myself from comment. 'Feasible' was just a question of finding the money, and governments always have difficulty with that, but denying the justice of the case for compensation was very hard to take.

Mr Alison then referred to the Royal Commission on Compensation and Civil Liability which had just been set up and said that the most constructive course to undertake in pursuing the question of compensation for vaccine damage was to give evidence to the Commission. He then spoiled what little hope there was by adding that the Prime Minister had made it clear that 'no recommendation the Commission might make could have any retrospective effect'.

Over the years, one learns that Parliamentary debates are intended to raise issues which the Government may later consider in detail, but that they do not produce firm answers to begin with. On that night, however, I was extremely upset and disappointed by Mr Alison's comments and I left the House of Commons even more determined to continue with what I knew was an entirely justified campaign for children severely damaged by vaccination. I was disappointed that the Royal Commission would obviously not provide any answer for us but was happy to know that Jack Ashley would act as our spokesperson in Parliament. He was the leader of many MPs who eventually supported our campaign, and it was through his efforts and those of his colleagues that we'd eventually succeed.

I spent that night in London with David's Aunty Betty who made me supper, helped me to wash all the makeup off my face and listened with interest to the details of the debate. I used her phone to ring David and to tell him what had happened. As usual he was at home babysitting two of our daughters: I had been able to arrange overnight accommodation for Helen at her day centre overnight facility.

6

Going to Press

Before the debate in Parliament, there had been some media interest in our campaign and a number of parents had told the stories of the damage to their children. When details of the Parliamentary debate were published, however, the press interest increased and television producers also became interested.

Appearing on television was a novel experience for me and I was always surprised by the different approaches to the story of vaccine damage. Some producers were very interested in the story and wanted to allocate a long programme to go into the matter in detail. Some wanted a quick fill-in in a general health programme and some wanted a quick item in a news programme.

Taking part in the interviews invariably involved a lot of travelling. I can remember occasions when I had to drop everything to appear on a programme in London or Manchester or locally in Birmingham. At that time in the 1970s, there was more money available for the making of programmes and it was quite usual for a taxi to be sent from London to Shipston on Stour to take me down and bring me home – all in a matter of about five hours. The same was true of radio programmes, most of which were done from the Pebble Mill studios in Birmingham; if I agreed to travel there myself, a small cheque to cover my time and expenses would follow, or otherwise the studio would send a taxi. Apart from the convenience of all this, it meant that one could be quite sure that an interview had definitely been arranged and that the journey was not a waste of time.

Times have changed. On two occasions in the 1990s, I rushed to Birmingham to take part in what I was assured was an important interview, only to find subsequently that the journalist in question had decided to do something different, without feeling obliged to let me know. Since this can be a waste of time and also a costly exercise, such an attitude can be very annoying.

I was never comfortable in television interviews. Sitting under the glare of studio lights, with a camera staring at me, made me feel extremely tense. Television interviewers varied from programme to programme and, although most were helpful and courteous, some were difficult. I particularly remember one interviewer who, while taking me into a studio, asked me, 'Why are you looking for money now that the damage had been done?' I sat speechless through the interview and afterwards asked him if he knew any disabled children or what the cost of their care was and whether, if anything happened to his children, he was in a position to provide care for life for them. He was upset at the comment about his own children but nevertheless failed to understand what I was talking about. I didn't agree to be interviewed by him again.

Radio interviews, on the other hand, were quite different. A small studio was provided with a radio link to the programme in question and I could sit in comfort and alone, with headphones connecting me to the interviewer at the other end. These interviews flowed effortlessly.

The first programme to become interested in the campaign for vaccine-damaged children after Jack Ashley's debate was *This Week*, a current affairs programme which went out nationally at the time. Initially, this was to be a programme about the campaign itself but, subsequently, the producers decided to make it a programme about compensation and they gathered up relevant information from me and from European sources. The programme went out on 4 April 1974, entitled *Public Safety – Private Risk: Vaccination*, following a preview on 3 April to which Jack and Pauline Ashley, Dr John Wilson and I were invited.

The programme told the story of one of Dr Wilson's patients, Keith Stokes, whose father Roy has since continued to fight for the rights of all vaccine-damaged children. At the time Keith was 11 years old and the

51

programme showed the extent of his disability following a severe reaction to vaccination when a baby. To highlight the question of compensation, the programme also showed a child in Germany, also severely disabled following vaccination, and referred to the fact that, in Germany, vaccine-damaged children received an allowance of £100 a month, a sum which would be increased as the children got older.

The Medical Officer of Havant was interviewed and confirmed that he was getting reports from doctors and from hospitals about small children crying, screaming and having fits after vaccination. He had investigated, he said, and found that this was likely to happen when the triple vaccination which included whooping cough vaccine was used and less likely to happen after the double, which was diphtheria and tetanus only.

Dr Wilson referred to his own recently published study of children admitted to Great Ormond Street Hospital with a severe illness within 24 hours of inoculation.

Dr Ehrengut, the German specialist who campaigned for the withdrawal of whooping cough vaccine in Germany, said he was quite convinced that whooping cough vaccinations should be stopped immediately because the number of vaccination victims equals at least, or even exceeds, the injuries due to the whooping cough disease itself.

Dr Ehrengut was head of Hamburg's immunological services at the time and the programme-makers travelled to Hamburg to talk to the parents of Andreas Lonski, a child who suffered irreparable brain damage following a severe reaction to whooping cough vaccine. His damage was very obvious and made quite an impact on those watching the programme. The difference between his case and that of Keith Stokes was that compensation of £100 per month was paid to the Lonski family to help care for Andreas while Keith's parents were left to bear the cost alone.

As Keith's mother and father said, 'If compensation can be won because of his own right of being an individual having being born normally, and then damaged accidentally, irreparably, then we feel that this is a right that he is entitled to as a human being.'

The programme was powerful, but concentrating as it did on the damage suffered by Keith and Andreas, I felt that its effect would be to stop whooping cough vaccination without having much impact on the compensation issue, and I said as much in the discussion programme which followed. This opinion was not very well received by the programme reporter, Peter Williams, but it did, in fact, prove to be the case. The day following the programme, according to an item in *Medical World*, hundreds of doctors telephoned the Department of Health asking about the whooping cough vaccination programme and, in the following year or two, the acceptance rate for the vaccination fell drastically until it reached only 30% in some parts of the country.

Later on, and even to this day, all of us involved were accused of being responsible for the drop in acceptances for whooping cough vaccination, which it was said led to large-scale epidemics of the disease, with many deaths. This was an unfair accusation as it was quite clear from the health experts involved that there was disquiet about the vaccination, largely hidden from the public until then, and the question really was whether this was a morally acceptable way of proceeding with a health policy.

It was also an untrue accusation as a study of the figures of whooping cough cases and deaths resulting from them in the following years shows that although there was a reported increase in the incidence of the disease, there was little if any increase in the number of deaths. As one medical expert said, doctors tend to report whooping cough in every child with a severe cough who has not been vaccinated, and the higher reported incidence of the disease at the time when the acceptance rate for the vaccination was very low was most likely biased to some extent.

The *This Week* programme was the start of many similar programmes about whooping cough vaccination and vaccine-damaged children over the following years. It also was the start of discussions about vaccine damage in other countries, particularly in America and Australia.

An American television crew came over to do an in-depth interview similar to the *This Week* programme, and American parents then wrote to ask for details of our campaign. Later, they set up a group called Dissatisfied Parents Together (DPT), the initials being taken from the diphtheria pertussis tetanus components of the triple vaccine. Campaigning continued in America until, with the help of Senator Edward Kennedy, the National Childhood Vaccine Injury Act was passed some years later. Campaigning also continued in Australia but no special scheme for vaccine damage resulted. Australian authorities discussed instead following the example of New Zealand, which had introduced the first comprehensive 'no fault' compensation scheme in the world for personal injury by accident.

The 1974 Parliamentary debate and the *This Week* programme launched the campaign in this and other countries for State responsibility for damage resulting from vaccination. We had achieved a certain amount of success in raising the issue, and in stimulating a debate into the public arena, but there was still a great deal to do if our goals were to be achieved.

7

Castle's Door Opens

For four years after his first debate in January 1974, Jack Ashley kept up a constant barrage of Parliamentary Questions and debates and there is no doubt that it was his persistence which eventually broke down the reluctance of the Government to introduce legislation which was seen by many to be controversial. The constant cry of the Government Departments was that any deviation from the policy of equal benefits for all disabled people could open the floodgates, with serious implications for Government finances, a theme which was adopted by the Conservative Government which followed in 1979.

After his January 1974 debate, which was just before the General Election in that year, an Early Day Motion (EDM) was put down under the names of Jack Ashley, Dr

Tom Stuttaford, Mrs Barbara Castle, Mr John Astor, Dr David Owen and Mr Ernie Money, calling on the Government to pay compensation to vaccine-damaged children. Some Members of Parliament say that EDMs are not very effective, but there is no doubt that when they are signed by influential Members they do put significant pressure on the Government. The importance of this particular EDM became obvious when, after the election, Labour were returned to power and Barbara Castle became Secretary of State with Dr David Owen as Minister of State, Department of Health and Social Security. Added to that, Jack Ashley had been appointed as Parliamentary Private Secretary to Mrs Castle. Although it meant that he would not be able to take part in any public debates – a discipline of the House of Commons to which he refers in his book *Journey into Silence* – it meant that he was now able to be influential behind the scenes and he quickly asked for and was given an appointment for me to meet with Barbara Castle to talk to her about our campaign.

Rene Lennon and I travelled down by train and took a taxi to the DHSS offices at Elephant and Castle. We were shown into a small office and asked to wait until the Minister was ready to see us. It was some indication of our naïevty and lack of experience in meeting Government officials that we sat whispering about what we would say and wondering if we were being observed.

I found the meeting, which took place on 10 May 1974, fascinating. Mrs Castle was, as usual, immaculately dressed. She wore a cream silk blouse with a tan suit, which set off her auburn hair, and her make up was perfect. She sat behind a large desk with her officials and advisers standing in a row at her right-hand side. I wondered whether they always had to do that and how tired they might become if the interview lasted for any length of time. It struck me as being a slightly autocratic habit, but no doubt it was one which was not unusual at the time.

The chairs in front of her desk had been arranged so that one was directly in front of her – which I assumed was for me as spokesman – while I assumed that the one to the side was for Rene. However, because Jack, who was her Parliamentary Private Secretary at the time, was standing at the far side with the advisers, I decided to sit in the chair to the side of the desk so that I could see him and note his reaction. Instead of telling me to move back, Mrs Castle continued to direct her comments and answers to Rene while I spoke from the side. It was a ridiculous situation I thought and I wondered about the inflexibility of such an approach.

We talked about vaccine-damaged children and I showed her a recent press cutting of a baby in Wales who had died within a short period of a severe reaction to his first vaccination, stressing the need for an investigation into the vaccine and help for the children already damaged. When I mentioned our aim at the time – to get some kind of insurance for the immunisation scheme which would provide for damaged children – Mrs Castle pointed out that insurance was not an answer as it would only be effective for damage occurring after it had been taken out. I think she could see that we were a novice group convinced of the rightness of what we were saying, but not always sure about how to proceed. At the end of the meeting I moved forward to the front of her desk to thank her for seeing us. It was then that she gave me what was to be the best piece of advice I was ever given, which was to go back to my office, make out the case for compensation, with professional help, if necessary, and then stick to that case in all interviews and official meetings.

That advice led me to prepare the *Case for Compensation for Vaccine Damaged Children*, an 11-page report based on whooping cough vaccination, the damage reported by parents and the confirmation of such possible damage in medical expert research. Whooping cough was chosen because it was the one blamed by three out of four parents for damage to their children.

Had it been some years earlier, the case might have been based on smallpox vaccination, damage from which was recorded by the Ministry of Health between the years 1951 to 1960 and which, despite the evidence of serious illnesses resulting from it, was still promoted until 1971.

The *Case for Compensation* was sent to Members of Parliament and Health Ministers on 13 August 1974. It was acknowledged by Dr David Owen, the Minister of State at the Department of Health, on 8 October 1974 as 'a clearly presented and moderately stated case for compensation which has much evidence on its side'. He went on to say that there was a Royal Commission studying the whole question of compensation, including that for vaccine damage, and that the Department's evidence to the Commission would take account of our case.

Barbara Castle had mentioned during our meeting that the Department was considering setting up 'a special sub-committee to review the information available on the risks of all immunisation procedures currently recommended', and when this committee was formed in May 1974 we all felt a sense of achievement. We had made our case and it had been well received and we had stimulated interest and concern into the vaccine, which was the source of much anxiety, not only among parents but among some medical experts as well.

It is true to say that I was not very popular with the Department of Health medical experts or their advisers for raising doubts about their immunisation progamme. The Association's *Case for Compensation* had been based on the details of whooping cough and, as we continued to get letters from parents blaming this vaccine, we clearly had to do something to bring the matter to the attention of the Government.

In January 1975, I wrote *The Story of Whooping Cough Vaccination* which included references to the expert research reports about damage from the vaccine published since 1948. Our report asked questions about the testing of vaccines, the lack of information to parents about possible risks and the lack of any acceptance of responsibility by the State when such risks materialised for individual children. The report was passed to the Department's expert advisory committee – The Joint Committee on Vaccination and Immunisation (JCVI) – who studied it and issued their comments, most of which were related to supporting the need to proceed with the vaccination and mentioning the proposed studies about which Barbara Castle had talked during our meeting. In their response to my request, the Secretary to the Committee said these studies 'would show' that the vaccine was safe and effective, which prompted my reply that if the study results were a foregone conclusion, there seemed to be little point in carrying them out.

The difference in attitude between the Department of Health Ministers and the medical experts who advised them on matters relating to vaccination and immunisation was very noticeable. These experts come from various medical disciplines, some of whom advised pharmaceutical companies who manufacture vaccines. Clearly, the knowledge they gain from such involvement helps them in their decisions when advising the Department of Health about vaccination programmes, but there was also the concern that they might be naturally drawn towards recommending certain drugs. It has been known for experts to sometimes speak to the media or go directly to the public to promote vaccination campaigns although they have no direct responsibility for or contact with the parents concerned. Expert advice is normally accepted by the Department of Health; there was an occasion in the 1970s during the debates about vaccine damage payments when expert advice was to set up a whooping cough vaccination campaign. David Ennals stopped this, which caused some consternation among the experts, but it was an inappropriate time for such a campaign. This was probably the only time a Minister over-ruled the experts.

Because of his duties as PPS to Barbara Castle, Jack was unable to follow on from his January debate, although other concerned MPs kept the issue in the public eye. In April 1974, Mrs Joyce Butler had put down an Early Day Motion urging a review of the vaccination programme and calling for a scheme of compensation along the lines of those in European countries. This motion attracted signatures from some who remained interested supporters of our campaign for the next 26 years, such as Dr Keith Hampson, Nicholas Winterton, William Ross, and from some who went on to become important members of the Government, such as Nicholas Ridley, Timothy Sainsbury, Alan Clark, Nigel Lawson and Neil Kinnock. Unfortunately, the prestige which we might have expected to remain attached to our work because of these names was short-lived as, once they became Ministers, they were no longer open to receipt of campaign correspondence.

In November 1974, there was a debate on Social Policy when Dr Owen confirmed that the question of vaccine damage would be referred to the Pearson Commission and that the Department would await the Commission's report before making any decision. This was followed up by an Early Day Motion by Kenneth Lomas, JPW Mallalieu and Ronald Brown, which again attracted much interest. Among the interesting names appearing on this Motion were those of Robin F Cook and Cecil Parkinson.

As 1974 drew to a close, I was left with the feeling that it had been a year filled with action and excitement. The membership of the Association had continued to grow, and I kept everyone informed of progress with fairly regular newsletters. Reading through those I issued at the time, I am reminded of the massive support which the campaign attracted in 1974. Early Day Motions put down in Parliament by Jack Ashley attracted numerous signatures, with many Members of Parliament writing to confirm their interest. Specialists who had published reports about vaccination, particularly whooping cough vaccination, including Professor Dick, Dr Brian Bower and Dr John Wilson helped enormously, and letters I wrote to Dr Schumacher, the specialist responsible for the German compensation scheme, brought helpful and encouraging replies. Medical journals such as *General Practitioner* and *World Medicine* published articles supporting the call for compensation and *The Lancet*, the expert source of medical reports and advice, joined in the call. 'Perhaps the responsibility of the State should be extended ... and responsibility for the rare case of disability following vaccination ... be accepted,' it wrote.

On the publicity side, John Stevenson of the *Daily Mail* took a special interest and published many helpful articles.

He also passed on to me articles of interest about Government reports and comments on vaccination and kept in touch regularly to remain focused on publicity angles. Then, one day, I could no longer reach him and only later discovered that he had died suddenly and tragically.

As a group of parents, we had a lot to talk about and a great deal to plan for the future, and we needed to see if any reorganisation of the Association was necessary. It had been set up on very informal lines with a simple statement of aims rather than a tight constitution, but one or two parents felt it should be formally set up with an enlarged and elected Committee with voting rights and rules.

Our first Annual General Meeting was called for the 7 September 1974 and was held at The Victory Services Club in Seymour Street, W2. Since we always considered that children damaged by vaccination in the interests of national health had something in common with soldiers damaged in the interests of national security, the Victory Services Club seemed an appropriate venue for our first meeting and for further meetings in the future.

Although the main purpose of the meeting was to get parents together and give them an opportunity to talk to others in a similar position, the meeting began with an attempt at formality. I presented the list of area secretaries for approval, and gave a report about the earlier meeting with Barbara Castle and the Department's response to our *Case for Compensation*. Our Treasurer, Catherine Hiatt, gave details of monies collected and held to cover the expenses of the campaign, mostly postage, telephone and travelling costs. Although her family was not included in our campaign, Catherine gave her time freely to help us and has continued to do so for many years. She also enlisted the help of an accountant who similarly gave his time freely to audit the accounts. He had originally given us the advice that we should only hold sufficient funds to enable us to pay the campaign expenses, and that as and when the funds were depleted we could then go back to the parents and ask for further small contributions. We took this advice and found that most parents were very generous when we mentioned the need for further subscriptions.

Alan Goff, who had been at our very first meeting in Birmingham, acted as Secretary and when the formal business was over we went down on to the floor of the hall to meet the parents and hear all their stories. It was a memorable day as I saw for the first time the impact which the creation of the Association was making. Parents from all over the country had come to London to talk to other parents with similar experiences and it was clearly an important day for all those involved. Everyone lingered over the tea provided by the Club and there was a constant buzz of conversation which went on late into the afternoon. In the end, we found it hard to tear ourselves away.

Up to the time our campaign started in late 1973, anyone who mentioned vaccine damage either to their friends, their GP, their social worker (if they had one) or anyone else connected with them and their disabled child had been regarded as peculiar, making them feel very much alone. The total of Association families listed at the time was 280, most of whom attended the meeting and found the opportunity to talk about vaccine damage to be a great relief.

There was talk, too, of the continuing reports of damage from whooping cough vaccine and parents wondered how best to raise this issue for the benefit of those parents currently worrying about vaccinating their babies. I told them that Jack Ashley intended to refer the matter to the Health Service Ombudsman, in order to bring some pressure to bear on the Department of Health experts who had yet to be convinced.

There had been an earlier proposal to set up a formal committee to act under a formal constitution, but it was not supported. Parents generally felt that, as a group of concerned parents acting together, anything which distracted us from the campaign itself would not help. Looking today at situations in which some committee members make controversial decisions about procedures and behaviour, about which the majority of their group members may be powerless to challenge, I think the parents made a wise choice.

The meeting transformed us from a large group known to each other only by letter or telephone, to a close body of parents acting together for a common cause. Parents left the meeting with renewed hope that, together, we could get the Government to consider their responsibility for the plight of our children and make special provision for them to enable us to cope with the burden of grief and disability which had followed the vaccination of our normal, healthy children.

Before they left, I told everyone that I believed we had two months to press the question of compensation legislation with the help of our MPs, believing then that something could be accomplished by December 1974 and that we would not have to wait for any recommendation from the Royal Commission.

During 1974, there had been prolonged publicity about our campaign. The matter had also been raised in Parliament by way of Early Day Motions which had attracted signatures from a large number of MPs. 150 Members of Parliament had written to express support for our aims, among them Sir Geoffrey Howe, William Whitelaw, Roy Jenkins, Michael Foot, Shirley Williams and many other influential Parliamentarians. We didn't see how we could possibly fail to achieve a quick solution but, with the benefit of hindsight and experience, it now seems as though our optimism was very naïve.

Between 1974 and 1976, MPs kept up a constant stream of questions to the Secretary of State about compensation and a number of Early Day Motions were tabled which got the support and interest of many Members of Parliament from all parties. There was still great concern about whooping cough vaccination and reports of damage were constantly being sent in by parents. In May 1976, when Jack Ashley was free again to lead the campaign, one of the first things he did was to ask the Ombudsman – The Parliamentary Commissioner for Health – to investigate the whole issue of how whooping cough vaccination was administered.

In the meantime, the Review promised by Barbara Castle had been initiated and three research studies were carried out by experts in the field over the following years. One was under the Chairmanship of Professor JA Dudgeon, Professor of Microbiology at the Institute of Child Health; another was under the Chairmanship of Dr TW Meade, Director of the Medical Research Council (MRC) Epidemiology and Medical Care Unit, and utilised data supplied in the main by our Association and Professor Stewart; and the third – the *National Childhood Encephalopathy Study* – was led by Professor DL Miller, Professor of Community Medicine at Middlesex Hospital Medical School.

Professor Dudgeon's panel noted several instances in which the vaccination had been carried out in the presence of a known contraindication and advised that the authorities concerned should provide information on the relevance of the conditions which would make vaccination unsafe. They stressed that there were limitations in examining cases retrospectively and said that the Committee on Safety of Medicines should collect full clinical, pathological and other data as soon as possible after a reaction was notified.

Dr Meade's panel also thought that examining cases retrospectively was unsatisfactory and was unsatisfactory for epidemiological purposes. They said, however, that this should not be taken to mean that pertussis (whooping cough) vaccine damage did not occur. The picture that emerged from the data gave a very strong impression that the vaccine was in these cases often responsible for the neurological events which followed.

The reports of these studies were published in the 1981 booklet *Whooping Cough – Reports from the Committee on Safety of Medicines and the Joint Committee on Vaccination and Immunisation*, and this document became instrumental in strengthening our campaign and exerting more pressure on the Government to deliver a satisfactory resolution.

8

Fault Findings

Jack Ashley spoke to Sir Idwal Pugh, the Parliamentary Commissioner for Health (the Ombudsman) who agreed to meet us at his offices in January 1977. He wanted clear details of what we considered to be faulty administration of immunisation programmes and, to provide this, I listed the vaccination details given to me by the parents of four children whose cases had been referred to the Association.

I spent a considerable amount of time collecting and preparing the cases but by 1977 I had a bit more freedom. Helen was now 15 and still attending her special day care centre where she not only received a high degree of care and attention from the staff but was now able to be cared for at night on occasions. The Manager, Hannalore, was particularly helpful and I could go away for special meetings leaving Helen in her care. So when Jack asked me to come down as soon as I could to meet Sir Idwal, I was able to arrange it and spend time beforehand typing up the details of the cases

The first case study involved Lisa, who was vaccinated at school at eight years old. She was given what was said to be a booster dose of tetanus, diphtheria and oral polio vaccines. There was no medical record of her previous immunisations available on the day and, had there been, it would have shown that this was, in fact, the first immunisation Lisa had ever had. Three days later, Lisa collapsed and had to be rushed to hospital, where doctors told her parents that at her age she should not have had what was, in fact, a primary vaccination.

Naomi's case showed how she had been vaccinated at 15 months old, shortly after having been discharged from hospital where she had been treated for an infectious disease. Naomi's parents had just moved home and went to an unfamiliar clinic where they mentioned the child's recent illness and hospitalisation. The medical records from the previous clinic had not yet arrived but, nevertheless, the clinic went ahead with a booster triple (diphtheria/tetanus/whooping cough) vaccination. Two days later, the child became paralysed, suffered convulsions and had to be readmitted to hospital.

The third case involved Stephen, who was hospitalised at two months old suffering from hydrocephalus, for which he had a valve inserted to drain fluid. When discharged, he made steady progress to the age of six months when he was given the first triple vaccination. During the following week, he collapsed twice and, on admission to hospital, was said to be suffering from a brain infection and was subsequently said to be brain damaged. Medical reports on the case suggested that the damage discovered was not that which was expected to be found after valve insertions.

The last case involved Khadine, a premature baby with a low birth weight. She was kept in hospital until she reached a weight of nearly 5 pounds, whereupon she was discharged but continued to be checked at intervals by the hospital and was due for a final progress check at six months. Shortly after discharge, when she was four months old – as computed from the date of her premature birth – she was 'called' for immunisation by a computer card, although she had not been seen by the Health Visitor, who was required to check her over before immunisation. Following immunisation, the baby was severely ill and at the next hospital visit – brought forward to five months because of concern for her condition – she was found to be brain damaged

These cases demonstrated a complete lack of concern about or knowledge of the rules regarding safe immunisation for young children, particularly those with medical conditions, which meant that immunisation should be either delayed or avoided. They also called into question the lack of information to parents about possible risks which could have helped them to protect their children.

The particular complaints were that the parents concerned gave their consent to the immunising of their children in ignorance of the risks to which this might be exposing them; there was also the fact that the parents' ignorance was caused by the failure of the Department of Health and Social Security to make available to those parents information about all the factors which they should have taken into account before they gave that consent.

The Ombudsman started his investigation in January 1977, carried out a very detailed study and presented his report to Parliament at the end of October 1977, which was titled *Parliamentary Commissioner for Administration; Sixth Report for Session 1976-77 — Whooping Cough Vaccination*.

The purpose of the investigation, the Ombudsman said, was to examine the administration of the policy about whooping cough vaccination since 1957 when it was first introduced into the national immunisation scheme. He studied, and commented on, the roles of all the various bodies involved in the immunisation process which included the Department of Health; the Joint Committee on Vaccination and Immunisation, which advised the Department; the Health Education Council, which was responsible for the publication of posters and leaflets promoting immunisation; the Committee on Safety of Medicines, whose function was to collect reports of any serious reactions to vaccines; and Health Authorities, who arranged for immunisation in their areas. He listed all the official and medical statements made and advice passed on to doctors.

The Department of Health told him that the responsibility for providing facilities for immunisation was a matter for Health Authorities and that the Department itself played no part in the process. The Department's view was that the final decision and responsibility for vaccination rests with the doctor.

The task of the Joint Committee on Vaccination and Immunisation, set up in 1962, was to advise the Secretary of State on all medical aspects of immunisation, taking into account published papers and studies from various medical and scientific sources. The Committee's advice is transmitted to doctors and Health Authorities. Until 1968, the advice made no reference to possible adverse reactions to vaccination.

The function of the Health Education Council was to prepare leaflets and posters promoting immunisation to parents at the request of the Department of Health. The leaflets did not offer any specific guidance to parents before 1976 when the first references to possible side-effects were included.

The Committee on Safety of Medicines had the task of arranging for the collection of reports of adverse reactions to vaccines from doctors who were asked to use a 'yellow card' system to make the reports. The system was a voluntary one and it was generally acknowledged that there was under-reporting.

While studying the role of Health Authorities, the

Ombudsman studied details of the immunisation of the four children referred to him and reported his findings in detail in his report.

The conclusions reached by the Ombudsman were that, whereas the Department of Health considered that it was for the doctor to decide about immunisation and the Department's job was only to transmit scientific and expert opinion down the channel to them, he considered their role and responsibility to be much more fundamental. He distinguished between the information a doctor gave to individual patients as part of his clinical duties, and the general health information which the Government provides for the public at large. He concluded that:

'The responsibility for the administration of policy on whooping cough vaccination rests squarely on the Department. I consider that they have not fully recognised this responsibility in the past...I consider that the Department must accept a large measure of responsibility and I believe that they should have recognised earlier the desirability of alerting parents, as they have now done.'

While not overtly criticising doctors, the report did note that the advice issued to them from 1963 should have been enough to alert them to the need for care and consideration in forming their clinical judgement, bearing in mind that the advice from the Department for Health and Social Security was not the only source of guidance available to them.

I clearly remember the morning the Ombudsman's Report was published. A number of press and TV Reporters came to my house to ask for a reaction and they were, as usual, in a hurry to get away to file their stories. Having just had time to skim through the report, and not having seen any specific reference to Government responsibility or what they owed by way of recompense to the damaged children, my initial comment, that the report was not likely to help our cause, was not fully justified. Later, from a detailed study of the report, I could see that the Ombudsman had clearly defined the duties of those responsible for immunisation and had found failures on the part of the Department of Health and doctors. Coming as it did just five months before the Royal Commission recommendation that the Government should be 'strictly liable' for vaccine damage, which was followed two months later by the announcement of the Vaccine Damage Payment Scheme, it is clear that the investigation by Sir Idwal Pugh played a very important role in influencing the Government both in relation to its responsibility for the safe promotion of vaccination and its duty to those who suffered in the process.

In his report, the Ombudsman said 'the Association have performed a valuable service in bringing this matter to the attention of the public and the authorities'. One specific area of significant improvement was in providing better information to parents –Health Education leaflets followed the Ombudsman's study and the very detailed booklets, such as *Immunisation Against Infectious Disease*, prepared for the guidance of doctors and nurses, are something of a revolution in the amount of detailed information given about vaccines and their production.

9

Royal Commission Responds

When we were told early in 1975 by the Government that 'no Minister in the Government can interfere in the matter of compensation until the Royal Commission reports' I felt it was clearly time to seek legal advice again.

While preparing the *Case for Compensation* earlier in 1974, I had asked John Hall, a Birmingham solicitor, for help. He had previously been asked by Rene Lennon to advise her about the possibility of legal action for Joanne – the girl whose story had appeared with Helen's in the *Birmingham Post* – and he helped us by reading our report to ensure that it made sense. He remained our adviser and a member of our Working Party for the remainder of the campaign.

He was unfailingly kind and always anxious to help in matters relating to the campaign. He gave all his time for free and needed only to cover whatever minor expenses related to his firm. The eventual success of the campaign for vaccine-damaged children owes much to his generosity in giving his time and support in the pursuit of our claim.

Following the Government's statement that our case would have to wait, John Hall's advice was that we should give evidence to the Royal Commission and argue for a scheme which would be retrospective.

It was at the same time that we discussed approaching the European Commission of Human Rights, and John Hall readily agreed that this would be a worthwhile additional exercise.

The Royal Commission for Civil Liability and Compensation for Personal Injury (known as The Pearson Commission) had been set up by the Government in March 1973 under the chairmanship of Lord Pearson following the Thalidomide tragedy. Its terms of reference were:

'To consider to what extent, in what circumstances and by what means compensation should be payable in respect of death or personal injury (including ante-natal injury) suffered by any person —

   a. in the course of employment
   b. through the use of a motor vehicle or other means of transport
   c. through the manufacture, supply or use of goods or services
   d. on premises belonging to or occupied by another or

e. otherwise through the act or omission of another where compensation under the present law is recoverable only on proof of fault or under the rules of strict liability having regard to the cost and other implications of the arrangements for the recovery of compensation, whether by way of compulsory insurance or otherwise.'

The Commission had been informed by the Govern-ment that any recommendations it made about compensation could not be retrospective, so we felt initially that giving evidence to it might not help the children for whom we were fighting. However, after advice from John Hall and from interested medical supporters, it was decided that there was nothing to be lost, and perhaps much to be gained, by giving evidence.

Another helpful professional supporter who joined in our work at that time was Dr John Wilson, consultant neurologist of Great Ormond Street Hospital for Sick Children and he accompanied John Hall and myself to give evidence before Lord Pearson, the Chairman of the Royal Commission, on the 11 April 1975.

The Commission was hearing evidence at their offices at 22 Kingsway in London. Their secretary, Miss Kebble, wrote to arrange the meeting, to tell me where the main entrance to the building was and to say that she or one of the assistant secretaries would be in the hall to meet us and take us to the conference room. Dr John Wilson, John Hall our legal adviser and I waited together and were then shown into a large room with a long table at the end of which sat Lord Pearson; his secretary and other Commission officials sat opposite and we sat facing them.

I had sent notes about our campaign and our ideas about compensation and we spent an hour answering questions from Lord Pearson and the Commission members and discussing our *Case for Compensation*, a copy of which we presented to them.

With Dr Wilson and John Hall beside me taking part in the discussions, I didn't feel nervous and was grateful that they were there to provide professional input. Although at the time we were not sure what the result of our meeting would be, there is no doubt that our attendance was important and resulted in the recommendation which came three years later that 'the authority concerned [with vaccination] should be strictly liable in tort for severe damage suffered by anyone, adult or child, as a result of such vaccination.'

The study by the Royal Commission was wide ranging: 252 meetings were arranged abroad, in North America, New Zealand, Australia and Europe; 225 meetings were held in the UK; the Commission received 865 written submissions from 766 organisations and individuals, and oral evidence was taken in the UK from 113.

The Report of the Royal Commission on Civil Liability and Compensation for Personal Injury was published in March 1978 in three volumes: (1) *Report*; (2) *Statistics and Costings*; (3) *Overseas Systems of Compensation*. An interesting note read that the total expenditure of the Commission was £1,337,446, of which £50,546 covered printing costs.

Chapter 25 was devoted to vaccine damage. This comprised an impressive list of all those who supported our call for compensation, including the British Medical Association, the Royal College of Physicians and Surgeons of Glasgow, the Royal College of Surgeons in Edinburgh, the Association of the British Pharmaceutical Industry and the British Insurance Association. It even included the Standing Medical Advisory Committee of the DHSS, and specifically mentioned that of all those who gave evidence about the need for compensation, 'nobody argued in the contrary sense'.

The Commission's conclusion was 'that there is a special case for paying compensation for vaccine damage where vaccination is recommended by a public authority and is undertaken to protect the community'.

Recommendation No.158 in the report was that 'vaccine-damaged children should, if severely handicapped, be entitled to the benefit which we propose for severely handicapped children generally. In addition, there is a special case for paying tort compensation [where there has been a breach of duty] for vaccine damage where vaccination is recommended by the State and is undertaken to protect the community; the authority concerned should be strictly liable in tort for severe damage suffered by anyone, adult or child, as a result of such vaccination.'

The benefit proposed for handicapped children generally was a non-taxable disability benefit of £4 per week payable from the age of two.

Regarding tort compensation, the report went on to

suggest that the basis of liability should be strict rather than based on fault, meaning that where it could be shown on the balance of probability that vaccination had caused injury, there should be compensation. The Commission was aware that proof of causation could pose problems for the Courts, but saw no need to suggest that the Courts should adopt a different approach to proof of causation than that of assessing the balance of probabilities as in the case of other tort actions.

Nine months before the publication of the Commission's verdict, James Callaghan, the Prime Minister at the time, had written to Lord Pearson to ask if the Commission would be dealing specifically with the problem of vaccine damage. On 9 June 1977, Lord Pearson replied that the Commission had 'indeed got very much in mind the problem of vaccine damage', although he could not say then what the recommendation would be. There was an almost immediate statement by David Ennals, Secretary of State for Social Services, that the Government had decided to accept in principle that there should be a scheme of payments for vaccine damage, applying to existing as well as new cases.

With the Commission's report now in print, the way was at last clear to opening the discussions with the Government about how vaccine-damaged children should be compensated for their injuries. It had taken us four years to get this far and it was just a small step forward. It was to be many long months yet before some provision for vaccine-damaged children became a reality.

10

Losing the Way in Europe

While maintaining our pressure on the Government and waiting for a recommendation from the Royal Commission, aware that if its recommendations were not retrospective, no provision for our children would result, we looked around for other ways to highlight our claim and continue to influence decision-makers in the Government.

Between our approach to the Royal Commission in 1975 and our case to the Ombudsman in 1977, most of my work was typing reports, writing letters and answering the phone. This didn't take up all my day and I began to feel like I wanted a change. Suzanne and Rosanna were at college and on the occasions I needed extra care for Helen I could call on a kindly neighbour who had got to know her and could look after her.

When I heard that there was a shortage of staff at our local social services offices I applied and started an interesting part-time secretarial job and stayed there for 18 months.

When the decision to approach the European Commission of Human Rights was taken I asked the Manager if I could use some office time to type out the application to the Commission and he readily agreed. The office had up-to-date equipment including electric typewriters – a welcome change from the manual typewriter I had been using up until then. The Manager and staff were fascinated by the details of my approach to the Commission and helped as much as they could.

I wrote to the Secretary of the European Commission of Human Rights in July 1975, asking for official forms on which to submit a case to the Commission and, with John Hall's help, I completed and sent these on the 9 August 1975. The application was acknowledged by the Commission Secretary on 28 August 1975 and given File No. 7154/75.

Cases to the Commission are dealt with in the order in which they become ready for hearing. Under their Rules of Procedure, a single member of the Commission, acting as Rapporteur, carries out a preliminary examination of the application and reports on the question of its admissibility to the plenary Commission. The decision taken about admissibility is given in writing to the applicant and there is a reminder that the Commission meets in camera and case files on applications and all correspondence and documentation are not to be made available to the public.

It was to be seven months before the Rapporteur could carry out his preliminary examination of our application in March 1976, and another two months before it could be considered among the list of cases for the Commission's session beginning in May 1976.

At the May 1976 Session, the Commission decided that notice of our Application should be given to the Government of the United Kingdom and that the Government should be invited to submit its observations in writing before the 30 July 1976. The Government's observations would then be sent on to me so that observations on them could be submitted.

It had now been a year since the approach to the Commission and it was becoming clear that there would be no quick response. Parents who had had their hopes raised by acknowledgement of the fact that vaccine damage was a reality, and wanted to have their claims about their children examined and decided upon, were becoming frustrated by the long wait for a solution.

With hindsight, of course, it is obvious that three years (from 1973 to 1976) was a very short time in which to change Government policy and medical opinion, but totally convinced, as all parents were, of the injustice of what had happened to their children and the urgent need to remedy this, we could not see any good reason for the long delay by the Government in reaching a decision. What we did not consider at the time was that the

Government needed the protection of something like a Royal Commission recommendation or a European Court ruling, to enable it to introduce what could be controversial provision for one group of disabled children.

Whether we liked it or not, we had to wait another year until January 1977 before the European Commission could move further on our claim. Six months previously, they had received the observations of the UK Government on our case and had sent these on for comment. The observations were related to the law about immunisation in the UK, stressing the voluntary nature of the procedure, the role of doctors in advising parents, and the requirement for manufacturers to keep records of reports of adverse reactions. There was also reference to the fact that help was available to all disabled children from sources such as the Family Fund.

Our case to the Commission had been made under Articles 2 and 8 of the European Convention on Human Rights. Article 2 covered 'everyone's right to life to be protected by law' and article 8 covered 'everyone's right to respect for his private and family life' but the Government argued that our case was about the 'quality of life', which was not covered by the Convention, and there was no 'intention' to cause injury as would be the case in a murder or deliberately injurious act. They stressed that vaccination was not compulsory and argued that our claim, based on these two articles of the Convention, was incompatible with the Convention, and was manifestly ill-founded.

In response to this, with the help of our legal and medical adviser, I prepared the Association's comments on the observations by the UK Government as to the admissibility of our application to the Commission of Human Rights. This was a 12-page document which identified many of the arguments which continue to be expressed today about routine immunisation in this country. For example, vaccination cannot be said to be truly voluntary if it is not available on request but is urged on parents by way of warnings about disease. The primary objective is the eradication of disease, which incidentally protects individuals, and the administration of the immunisation programmes is carried out in such a way as to create dangers for some children.

This Association report went back to the European Commission in September 1976 and we then hoped for a firm ruling as a matter of some urgency. We were left waiting, though.

Six months later, in March 1977, the Commission considered our application again and decided that they needed more information from the UK Government before they could proceed. Among other things, they asked the Government for more detailed statistics on the incidence of death and injury to children participating in immunisation schemes (which the Government was unable to provide); details of checks made to show whether there were any contraindications to immunisation (symptoms or conditions which indicate that it would be harmful to administer a vaccination) and if parents were asked to provide information to doctors about any such contraindications; and details of the roles of members of the medical profession in the administration of vaccination schemes.

It was clear that the European Commission investigated our complaint fully, but it seemed as though the only activity was the shuffling of mountains of documentation between Westminster and Brussels, resulting in us being no nearer to any helpful ruling on the only question of major importance to us – compensation for our damaged children.

We were now into 1977 and the Report of the Royal Commission, including a recommendation for strict liability for vaccine damage, had been published. Following the statement by David Ennals in June 1977 that the Government would introduce a scheme of payments, the European Commission wrote to ask if 'I would state my position' regarding my application because of Ennals' statement, but I confirmed that the application to the Commission would not be withdrawn until I was certain that our case had been answered.

Although it was confirmed by the Commission that the application would continue to be examined, I think a lot of the pressure to get a favourable ruling was lost. The Commission clearly thought, as did many others, that the statement from the Government implied a scheme of compensation based on the Pearson recommendation and, in fact, they made this clear in the Decision of the Commission which I received on 21 September 1978.

The Commission ruled that there was no provision in the Convention on Human Rights conferring a right to compensation for injury or damage in the cases we put forward. The Commission was satisfied that Article 2 was intended to cover taking life 'intentionally' and that this was not the case in immunisation programmes in which there was a possibility of adverse reactions. The Government did not 'intend' such adverse reactions and damage to occur.

In relation to Article 8, the Commission ruled there was no interference with the right to respect for private and family life and therefore there had been no breach of the Convention meaning that the question of a right to compensation did not arise. The State, it said, does not compel parents to vaccinate their children or be vaccinated themselves, either directly or indirectly, by imposing sanctions on those who refuse vaccination. The State, it said, provides vaccination for those who wish to avail themselves of the services offered and, in this respect, the Commission did not accept that the consent given by parents is not a proper consent.

It would be very interesting to see whether a similar ruling could be made by the Commission today at a time when doctors are being threatened with a reduction in their fees if they do not achieve vaccination targets, which results in parents being pressured by doctors. There are numerous reports of parents being told that if they do not agree to vaccinate their babies, they will be struck off the practice register, or that if their child gets the disease for which the vaccination was refused, the doctor is unlikely to be very sympathetic. There are also reports of vaccinations, particularly the MMR vaccination, being given 'by stealth', meaning that it is included with another vaccination without reference to the parent's stated wishes.

The Commission's final paragraph was later on misinterpreted by some parents as ruling that the Payment Scheme introduced by the Government in 1978 was an interim payment. It stated, 'The Commission notes the commitment of the Government in various statements made in Parliament to draw up a compensation scheme for vaccine-damaged children and to make a lump sum payment in the interim.' It was not, of course, surprising that the Commission should have reached such a conclusion, as everything that was said by David Ennals in Parliament both before and after the introduction of the Payment Scheme led everyone to believe that the payment 'was not the end and not wiping the slate clean'. However, for the sake of clarity, it was necessary to ask whether the statement by the Commission was part of their legal ruling or just a comment, and they confirmed in February 1981 that their legal ruling referred only to the evaluation of the legal merits of the case we put forward. Their comment about the possible compensation scheme was, like our own, wishful thinking.

The Decision from the Commission was received in July 1978 shortly after the Government had announced details of the £10,000 payment scheme promised in June 1977.

11

Breakthrough

E arly in 1977, four years after setting up the Association, the time had come to get parents together again to give them a full report on progress so far. The reality of vaccine damage had been established and whatever Government scientists and advisers said, Ministers were concerned. The Ombudsman had investigated cases of maladministration and had clearly laid the responsibility for the promotion of immunisation at the door of the Government, criticising some of their methods. The Committee on Safety of Medicines had expressed concern. The Royal Commission was about to issue its report and the Government was anxious to know what it had decided about compensation for vaccine damage. Prime Minister James Callaghan had written to the Commission for confirmation that a recommendation about compensation would be included in its report and had given a statement to the BBC *Nationwide* programme on March 24 1977 to the effect that vaccine-damaged children should be compensated. David Ennals had agreed to meet a number of Association parents and had expressed sympathy and concern for the case we were making.

About seven of the longest-serving members of the association came with me to the meeting which was held in a large committee room in the House of Commons. This had all been arranged by Jack Ashley who attended the meeting with us and arranged for us to have tea afterwards. David Ennals came in to the room with one or two other MPs and some of his officials and welcomed us all.

I was amused by an incident which occurred during the meeting. A loud bell sounded after which David Ennals, the MPs and the officials left the room and were away for some time. When they returned it was explained that what we heard was a division bell calling MPs to the House to vote. David Ennals then turned to the others to ask, 'What was it we were voting for?'

Evidently these votes are prearranged and I thought, If you have been told what to say there is no need to know what you are saying!

David Ennals and his advisers made it clear that our case was being taken seriously, that studies were underway to see how it could be answered and that we would be given details of their proposals before our next parents' meeting.

It had been a long, hard struggle but we finally felt that

our efforts had not been in vain and it was decided to get together at the Victory Services Club on 28 March 1977 to celebrate what we saw as our success. David Ennals had promised to let us have a statement before the meeting and we assumed this was to be a statement of intent about compensation. It was only later we were to realise that Ministers do not make policy statements in public, before they have made them in the House of Commons, and the statement which I received from David Ennals the night before our meeting was disappointing.

In 1977, there were no such things as fax or email messages, or any of the methods of communication which we take for granted today. The message from David Ennals, which is still in my file today, came by way of a telegram. The message was first telephoned to a Post Office operator who confirmed it by a telegram made up of typed tape stuck on to a telegraph form and posted on from the nearest telegraph office.

The message read:

'I PROMISED YOU AT OUR MEETING ON MONDAY THAT I WOULD GIVE YOU A STATEMENT WHICH YOU COULD READ OUT AT YOUR RALLY ON SATURDAY — STOP — I WAS IMPRESSED BY THE VERY STRONG CASE WHICH YOU MADE FOR PAYMENT OF COMPENSATION FOR DAMAGE SUSTAINED AS A RESULT OF VACCINATION — STOP — I SAID THAT I WOULD GIVE FURTHER THOUGHT TO ALL THAT YOU AND THE MEMBERS OF YOUR DELEGATION HAD SAID — STOP — IN VIEW OF THE EVENT OF THE PAST WEEK, I THINK YOU WILL UNDERSTAND THAT A LITTLE

MORE TIME IS NEEDED FOR THIS — STOP — I HOPE YOU WILL
APPRECIATE THAT IN THE CIRCUMSTANCES I CANNOT YET SAY
MORE THAN IN MY RECENT STATEMENT IN THE HOUSE OF
COMMONS — STOP — I ASSURE YOU THAT I AM CONSIDERING
MOST CAREFULLY THE CASE YOU HAVE MADE AND THAT I WILL
BE IN TOUCH WITH YOU AGAIN AS SOON AS I AM ABLE — STOP
   DAVID ENNALS'

The event of the past week to which he was referring was James Callaghan's statement on the BBC *Nationwide* programme. Although it was clear that there was Government support for our case and that we had almost won it, we were so impatient for a conclusion that we did not fully appreciate what David Ennals was saying. Our meeting went ahead on 28 March but it was not the happy occasion we had thought it would be.

I read out the telegram to loud expressions of disappointment and anger. Parents who had travelled from all over the country hoping to hear of a definite Government proposal were left with the impression that an uncaring Government was using excuses to delay or maybe refuse any settlement of their claim.

I was able, however to read to them the details of the three recent debates, two in February and one in March 1977, in which Jack Ashley had taken part and in which he had attacked the Secretary of State for giving false figures of those damaged by whooping cough vaccination and for failing to take urgent steps either to protect other children from such damage or make provision for those already damaged. Jack had also written to the Prime Minister, James Callaghan, asking him to receive a deputation of parents together with MPs.

All parents present were asked to write again to the Secretary of State to tell him of the damage done to their children and their determination to continue a fight for compensation. It was also suggested that there should be a lobby of Parliament by a number of parents and the date set for this was 6 July 1977.

The meeting with the Prime Minister and the lobby of Parliament were forestalled by the letter which the Prime Minister wrote to the Pearson Commission on 6 June 1977 asking for an assurance that the Commission would be dealing specifically with the question of vaccine damage to which Lord Pearson replied that the Commission 'has indeed got very much in mind the problem of vaccine damage'. He went on to say that all had reached the conclusion that some kind of financial assistance should be made available for very serious injury resulting from vaccination recommended by a public health authority.

Although I was sorry to have missed the opportunity of meeting the Prime Minister, I was not sorry that the public lobby of Parliament became unnecessary. Rightly or wrongly, I have always felt that lobbies by letter are more effective: A few hundred letters circulating among Members of Parliament who will have time to read them, respond to them and take action on them in Parliament to my mind creates a long-lasting impact and continues to involve the MP over a longer period.

I have also always thought that groups of parents attending public gatherings can be deeply upset when they find that, however sympathetically they are listened to, no solution to their grievance is offered. The anger and frustration to which this leads can far outweigh any consolation which they hoped to gain from the meeting. I also know that whereas some parents willingly go to group lobbies with their disabled children, many would not consider involving their children in this way. I have been criticised for this attitude and regarded as a less effective campaigner because of it, but I still believe that 'the pen is mightier than the sword' and inflicts less personal damage.

On 14 June 1977 came the statement in the House of Commons for which we had patiently waited for so long. Referring to the reply that James Callaghan had received from Lord Pearson, David Ennals said, 'I am glad to inform the House that in the light of the conclusion which the Royal Commission has reached, the Government have decided to accept in principle that there should be a scheme of payments for the benefit of those who are seriously damaged as a result of vaccination, and that it will apply to existing as well as new cases.' He added that the detailed provisions of the scheme and the criteria to be established could not be determined until the Commission's report had been received and studied.

The welcome statement, confirming as it did that our campaign had succeeded and our claim had been vindicated, nevertheless maintained the suspense under which we had suffered for so long. There was no indication of when the Royal Commission Report would be published or what it would recommend by way of a scheme of payments. All we did know at that time was that it would be a retrospective scheme and would benefit all those vaccine-damaged children for whom we had campaigned.

It was very frustrating and created a lot of extra work for me. There were constant requests from parents for information which I did not have and I had to keep on writing to MPs to ask them to raise questions in Parliament. I had to leave my job at social services and devote more time to campaign correspondence.

Then my mother in Ireland became ill and I went to visit her twice, regretting that I couldn't stay for any length of time. When I had told her earlier of the progress of our campaign she had written to say she was glad that there was light at the end of the tunnel – but sadly she did not live to see it.

Parliamentary questions in July 1977 from Jack Ashley and other interested Members of Parliament attempted to find out from David Ennals when he would be able to advise parents about the scheme of payments or if he would announce some guidelines soon. It was one thing to be assured that there would be payments, but another to be left in the dark for a long period about the details, and Members of Parliament were concerned to try to give their constituents any information they could glean from the Government.

However, all queries brought the answer that there would be no details until the Pearson Report was published and available for study, and this did not happen for almost another year. *The Report of the Royal Commission on Civil Liability and Compensation for Personal Injury* was 'presented to Parliament by Command of Her Majesty' in March 1978, following which the Prime Minister made a statement confirming the recommendation about vaccine damage and, two months later on 9 May 1978, David Ennals made the long-awaited statement about the payment scheme.

'The Royal Commission has recommended firstly that in future there should be strict liability in tort for severe damage suffered by anyone as a result of vaccination which has been recommended in the interests of the community; and secondly, that there should be a new weekly benefit for all seriously disabled children whatever the source of their handicap. These and other considerations are being considered carefully by the Government. But this is bound to take time and, in view of the clear undertaking we have given in respect of vaccine damage, the Government have decided to bring forward urgently a scheme of payments.'

This became the Vaccine Damage Payment Scheme 1978. The payments came nowhere near meeting the recommendation for strict liability, neither did the

Payment Act which followed in 1979. But as a gesture of help to parents who had been caring so long for their seriously injured children, it was welcomed by all as a first step.

Announcing the scheme on 9 May 1978, David Ennals said,

'The scheme will provide for the payment of a lump sum of £10,000, tax free in respect of those, whether children or adults, who have since 5 July 1948 been severely damaged as a result of vaccination which has taken place in the United Kingdom against diphtheria, tetanus, whooping cough, poliomyelitis, measles, rubella or tuberculosis (BCG) or smallpox up to the date when its routine use ceased to be recommended.

'In the interests of speed and ease of administration, we shall accept, as the initial but not the exclusive, criterion of severe damage the receipt of attendance or mobility allowance for conditions which could be attributed to vaccine damage. Decisions whether the severe damage was due to vaccination will be made on the balance of probabilities. There will be a right of appeal to an adjudicating body, made up of two medical specialists and a legal chairman, which would be fully independent.'

Adding that the scheme would cover existing as well as any which might occur while it continued in operation,

David Ennals stressed that bringing the payment forward did not in any way pre-empt decisions which had to be made on the Royal Commission's recommendations as a whole.

The statement produced great excitement among the parents and the media. My telephone started ringing at around 6.00pm after the news was broadcast and it continued to ring until about 2.00am the following morning, until it eventually stopped working. I didn't have a mobile, or a walkabout phone in those days, and had to sit at the end of the stairs taking one call after another. The relief of finally making a breakthrough in our campaign initially took over from all other considerations and, to begin with, everyone was pleased. After four-and-a-half years of constant pressure I was very relieved. I knew there would be work to do to get the payments set up and, afterwards, to plan for continuing the campaign to get a better settlement, but for the time being I could relax and enjoy the success of my efforts, and those of all our other supporters and helpers who had made such an outcome possible.

It wasn't until the next morning that I could ring my closest colleagues and friends to talk about the good news. Everyone saw it as a great breakthrough in a hard battle and I was somewhat overcome by their congratulations and praise, because the focus of my concern was Helen in particular.

Something always turns up to spoil things. That morning I got really tired of the phone ringing and put it under a cushion so that David and I could try to have our breakfast in peace. I knew that it was ringing but ignored it for a while. When I answered, a very irate TV reporter asked why it had taken me so long to answer and went on to tell me very crossly that 'she had an important job to do and wasn't very happy about being kept waiting.' I don't remember much about that interview!

12

Making It Happen

Before David Ennals' statement, there had been discussions with the officials responsible for drawing up the scheme and some arguments about their interpretation of Pearson's reference to treating all disabled children equally. As is very clear from the Commission's Report, Pearson drew a distinction between those who could prove the cause of their injury and those who could not, and having said that all those who could not show cause (including those vaccine damaged) should get the weekly benefit he proposed, he added the recommendation of strict liability 'for those who can be shown to have been the victims of vaccine damage'.

Under such a scheme, parents would be able to go to Court to pursue their claims. There would be no need to claim negligence on the part of the Government or Health Authority concerned, but it would have to be proved that the vaccine caused the damage.

Pearson felt that this should not be impossible and that the same rules governing proof on the balance of probability in other cases should suffice. However, in the 26 years since, causation in vaccine-damage cases has never been established. Proof requires scientific studies which can demonstrate precisely how the vaccine, when injected into the body, leads to a reaction which causes severe damage and, although many suppositions and theories have been voiced, there has been no scientific answer. Until such time as there is, successful court action in these cases will not be possible.

Referring to the amount of any payment, the first proposal was £5,000 and I well remember telling a Social Security official on the phone that if he wanted to make a laughing stock of the department he should say that publicly. He wasn't at all friendly and obviously had no interest in what was, after all, an interesting new development. Of course, it wasn't in his power to decide the amount of the payment so I told him I would take the matter up again with his Minister, David Ennals. He obviously reported back my reaction because they then had second thoughts and said it would be £10,000, which I tried to argue about but I was told that as soon as a payment had been mentioned, there had been a flood of applications for it from all over the country which were already being processed. In a situation like this, it is not possible to organise a boycott of the offer in order to get a better settlement.

To begin with, therefore, everything was concentrated on discussing the payment in detail, finding out how parents' claims should be made, what arrangements would be made for making the payments, and how Deeds of Trust would later be drawn up. The Association was involved at all stages in these discussions and met the officials involved on a number of occasions to iron out some problems and suggest certain improvements.

At the time, I held on file about 1,200 letters from parents who felt their children had been damaged by vaccination and were entitled to the payment. In approximately 600 of these cases, parents had completed a detailed questionnaire which had enabled me to regard them as Association members with good grounds for a claim of vaccine damage. In all other cases, I had written to the parents to say that I would hold their details on a separate file but that this would not make them any less important and that I would pass them on immediately to any official investigating body as and when a payment scheme was set up.

A simple standard of proof was set by the Government for claims under the Vaccine Damage Payment Act. There needed to be proof of vaccination, evidence of a severe reaction reported at the time, evidence that the reaction took place within the time and in a manner which experts in immunisation regarded as a reaction and no evidence of any other illness which could have caused the damage.

At the meetings with officials, I was asked to hand over all these letters and questionnaires to the Vaccine Damage Payment Unit which I did following a letter to Association members asking for their consent. Nobody refused, although, later, one or two people said they could not remember the consent form and wanted their details returned, which is probably an inevitable event in such cases.

It was initially decided that part of the £10,000 would be put in Trust for the damaged child and part would be paid directly to parents who have, Mr Ennals said, 'to bear the burden of the day'. The question of what proportion to put in Trust was a matter which had to be considered carefully, he said, and would be part of the ongoing discussions with the Association and its advisers. As it later transpired, this was one of the difficulties which had to be resolved during the discussions. Ministers can promise whatever they feel to be appropriate but when the details get down to the officials and lawyers, it becomes a different matter. Handing over some of the money to parents to spend as they wished conflicted with what Government lawyers saw as a strict interpretation of the rules relating to Trust fund monies for the benefit of severely disabled people unable to manage their own affairs.

On the day this was being discussed, John Hall, our legal adviser, and I argued that Parliament had promised that the parents who had long borne the costs of caring for their vaccine-damaged children would be given some refund of their costs, but the difficulty of arranging this was seen to be insurmountable. Later, when I left the meeting so that the solicitors could carry on discussing the legal niceties, I spent some time worrying about how to resolve the dilemma over a contribution for parents and it suddenly occurred to me that parents could, quite rightly, have started to make purchases for their disabled child as soon as they were sure that a £10,000 payment would be forthcoming. I contacted the DSS officials asking them to include a clause in the Deed of Trust giving parents the right to repay themselves anything they had spent from the date on which the announcement of the payment was made in Parliament, 9 May 1978, to which they agreed and which solved the problem. This clause has remained part of all Deeds of Trust to the present day.

Although eventually it was seen that the Deed of Trust gave fairly wide-ranging powers to parents to spend money for their disabled children, and that concern about including a clause to cover family costs may have been somewhat unnecessary, the fact remains that most parents would feel guilty about using any of the money to benefit themselves unless clearly authorised to do so.

Discussions between the Association's Working Party and the DHSS officials went on until July 1978, covering questions such as putting the money in Trust, children of parents serving in the Forces vaccinated abroad, rubella vaccination of adults, children who died before the 1978 statement, and partially disabled children. After July 1978, the drafting of the Deed of Trust became a matter for discussion between the Department's legal team and John Hall, and my job was to make sure that all letters and reports from parents went to the Vaccine Damage Payment Unit, set up in Blackpool, so that the work of putting the payments in hand could begin.

Payments began to be made in early 1979 from the office in Blackpool set up by the Department. The Association was then invited to discussions with Department officials to help with passing on claims from families and to comment on the provisions of the Deed of Trust under which the payments would be made. John Hall accompanied me and Rene Lennon to the meetings and we were satisfied that we were able to represent any anxieties and queries which families had. The discussions continued until the plans to ratify the Payment Scheme by the introduction of the Vaccine Damage Payment Act were announced in February 1979.

In all the discussions, the civil servants involved were helpful and considerate. They were anxious to set up meetings and have all the issues resolved as urgently as possible and it was only later, talking to one of the officials, I realised that if things had not been finalised before May 1979, when the election returned a new Conservative Government, we would probably have ended up with nothing.

Parents continued to be critical of the amount of the payment, a criticism which was often repeated in Parliament by their MPs. Compared to the cost of providing for a severely disabled, vaccine-damaged child for life, the amount was minimal and many said it should have been at least ten times the initial figure. However, the Government was deaf to all arguments and the Payment Act covered only the sum of £10,000.

What saved the situation, although it was to take years to be effective, was the statement David Ennals made when announcing the payment originally – 'This is not saying this is the end – we are wiping the slate clean … This is some way in which we can help these people now…'

With these words and that promise, we were able to continue to say that the Government owed us a 'debt of honour' which we wanted them to pay.

The Vaccine Damage Payment Act to cover the Payment Scheme was passed following Statements in the House of Commons on 5 and 15 February 1979.

Although a £10,000 payment was less than what could be regarded as compensation, it was still a help and created a position which was much better than that which had existed four years earlier, when no one talked about vaccine damage or took responsibility for the children who were suffering.

It was quickly decided to get on with the business of arranging the payment by discussions with the Department rather than waste time arguing. There had been the suggestion from a few parents that we should refuse to accept the £10,000, but it was quickly pointed out that such a tactic would fail unless every family took part and it would not be in the best interests of most of the families, who had long waited for help, to endorse such a suggestion.

When the Vaccine Damage Payment Act was passed on 15 February 1979, all of us who had fought so hard for vaccine-damaged children felt proud of our achievements. Our small local committee which had come together in Birmingham was jubilant. There was Alan who had acted at meetings as our Secretary; Catherine who had kept our accounts; Rene who had helped with research; there were all those who had taken on the job of area secretary; and Helen in Scotland who had kept the parents there in touch. Without all of them, my job would have been impossible and the campaign itself would never have been such a success in such a short time We had not only got an acknowledgement of responsibility for vaccine damage from the Government, but we had also done much to highlight the risks to some children from vaccination procedures. The Debate on the Act in the House of Commons was attended by many Members of Parliament from all parties who had supported us in our campaign, all praising the measure which would benefit their constituents and referring to it as a magnificently humane Bill, despite its shortcomings regarding the amount of the payment. Jack Ashley, while acknowledging that 'David Ennals had introduced a measure which will be warmly welcomed throughout the country' reminded the House that the Bill was a 'stop-gap', and expressed the hope that it was the precursor of a far greater measure and one which would adequately recompense the families concerned.

There was also widespread media reporting of the details. Of course, a lot of the excitement about the payment had worn off because of the statements the previous year but the debate answered many of the questions being asked about regulations and procedures.

Referring to the campaign by The Association of Parents of Vaccine Damaged Children, which I had led for the previous six years, I was proud when David Ennals said, 'it was one of the best examples I have experienced of a group of people with a cause that they know is right changing the course of events. They achieved results because of the way they campaigned. They did not cause any antagonism ... They have been responsible, helpful, forthright and wise ... Their campaign was almost a perfect example of how a voluntary organisation should do its job.'

I had always felt that preparing a strong argument and pursuing it effectively with the help of influential support was the best way to campaign, although it may take a bit longer to achieve a result. On the other hand, shouting from the rooftops and verbally abusing the people being asked to answer a complaint may have more dramatic impact but, however successful, it creates a bitterness which can spoil the result.

It goes without saying that without Jack Ashley in Parliament to promote the arguments and keep up the pressure on the Government, the result might have been very different and we might never have had a Payment Act on which to build for better compensation later. Jack was warmly congratulated by MPs from all sides of the House during the debate with one MP recording the fact that the success 'was very much due to the efforts of the Hon Member for Stoke-on-Trent, South – Mr Ashley, who had spearheaded the Thalidomide campaign and followed it up with the campaign for vaccine-damaged children; he had suffered some abuse from writers and others in the media (for talking about vaccine damage) and even had some difficulties with the Government in exchanges in the House. Nevertheless, he stuck to the campaign and spearheaded it and he must be feeling proud of the outcome today.'

While many Association parents saw the £10,000 payment as a help and were determined to keep on campaigning to get it increased, there were some who saw it as a failure. At a parents' meeting which had been held the previous November, there were demands that 'we fire our advisers and get better ones', without making any suggestions as to how we could pay for expert legal and medical help to replace that which had been given voluntarily. There were demands to send aggressively worded letters to the Ministers involved and, although it was not said out loud, it was indicated that perhaps a better leader of the campaign should be found who would proceed more forcefully. As these were a very small minority of the total membership and, knowing that in any group there is always someone who is dissatisfied, I wasn't too surprised. Certainly £10,000 was not a reasonable sum to compensate for the damage but it was, as I and others thought, a good start and something to build on for a better payment later. I found it hard to understand the attitude of people who were criticising what had been achieved, when only four years previously there had been no hope of any help and they had never had recognition of the cause of their children's illnesses. A few of these parents carried on their grievance for another twenty years and then decided to support another later campaign. However, the majority of parents said they would continue to campaign in hope.

We now had to try to work together to get a more appropriate settlement for our vaccine-damaged children. The possibility of taking legal action as a way of obtaining proper compensation was now discussed. It was pointed out that such action could only be brought where negligence concerning vaccination can be established and where it could be scientifically proved that the vaccine had caused damage. It appeared at the time that only a minority of Association parents had possible grounds for legal action and they were advised to appoint their own solicitors to carry out initial investigations.

For everyone else, the most important question at the time was when the Payment would be made and what conditions, if any, would be placed on its use, and the meeting ended with a decision to meet again when the situation had been clarified.

Parents were advised to seek any professional help or

advice they needed while pursuing their claims, and this upset one or two people who felt that 'the Association' should provide the necessary help. Of course, the reality of 'the Association' was that it was just a name given to the group of parents who were similarly motivated to pursue a campaign. There was no care/welfare/advice role, and neither were there ever the funds or personnel available in order to undertake such a role.

Merely having a group title which becomes listed in various reference indexes attracts numerous requests for information, advice and help, and it can be difficult to explain the reality of the role. All such requests from people outside the organisation create costs that a small campaign fund cannot easily cope with, and I often wished there was some public way of reminding people to enclose a stamped, addressed envelope with their queries. Some people were very thoughtful in this respect, but there are hundreds of students every year seeking information on specific subjects and, although replying was costly, I found it difficult to refuse those who wanted to know about vaccination.

Once all the letters and details I had on file from parents had gone to the DHSS and arrangements for the start of the payments had been made, there was time to think about the amount we were to get and its relevance in terms of our campaign for compensation.

There were rumours at the time of a forthcoming election. Dr Vaughan, the Conservative Spokesman for Health, had written to me when the Payment Act was passed to say that the Conservatives 'support the intention that all vaccine-damaged children should be covered and also that there should be proper compensation, rather than simply a payment for the very severely damaged'. I was therefore extremely confident that we would be able to persuade an incoming Conservative Government to finish the compensation scheme. Dr Vaughan had added in his letter, 'I hope you will maintain your campaign and let me know if I can help in any way.'

This was 1979, five years since the campaign had started, and the year I thought it would end, bearing in mind David Ennals' promise and Dr Vaughan's clear statement of support.

All our efforts would now be directed to getting the newly-elected Conservative Government to end the suspense that had been created for us when it was said the scheme of payments was 'not the end' and 'not wiping the slate clean', and since in Opposition their Health Spokesman had promised to support our efforts to get compensation, we didn't see how we could fail.

I didn't have to wait long to find out.

13

Broken Promises

When the 1979 election produced a Conservative Government, I was very happy. Patrick Jenkin became Secretary of State for Social Services and Dr Gerard Vaughan became Minister for Health. I had been in correspondence with Dr Vaughan for some time and he had been open in his support for what I was trying to achieve. It was only a few months before the election that he wrote to me to say he hoped the Vaccine Damage Payment Bill was going to be satisfactory, but if there was anything about it which worried me, I should let him know. He was sometimes able to come to an arrangement with the Government, he said, and had previously written similarly encouraging words of support to another Association member. He stated that he was able to support us as Mrs Thatcher herself had told him that she personally felt that compensation of some kind should be paid and she had appointed him as spokesman.

I didn't know Patrick Jenkin but assumed that, as Secretary of State, he would be fully aware of the views of his Minister for Health and, indeed, of his now Prime Minister.

I wrote to both Patrick Jenkin and Dr Vaughan early in June 1979 to point out the difference between what the Royal Commission had recommended for vaccine-damaged children and what had so far been given under the Vaccine Damage Payment Act. Since the £10,000 had been said 'not to be the end', I urged an early conclusion to the compensation scheme and asked for a meeting to discuss the matter.

Initially, Patrick Jenkin linked the compensation issue to the Royal Commission's report, saying that all the matters were still under consideration and the proposals about vaccine damage could not be taken in isolation. He felt it would be quite wrong to accept any claim about vaccine damage before completing his examination of the more general question of a future coherent system of cash payments for the disabled. He noted my request for a meeting to discuss the matter and agreed to arrange this.

A meeting at which Patrick Jenkin and Dr Vaughan were present was then arranged at which my colleagues and I hoped to convince them of the urgent need to finish the scheme of payments. Being overly anxious not to cause discord, I didn't ask Dr Vaughan about his previous letter and kept waiting for him to say something himself, which he didn't. So I decided I would ask him for a separate meeting at a later date.

Although we were courteously received, and listened to patiently, we got nowhere. Following that meeting on 24 October 1979, Patrick Jenkin wrote in great detail about the reasons for the Government's refusal to do anything more which, in brief, repeated what had been previously set out as Conservative policy – to improve provision for disabled people generally when resources permitted 'including those disabled as a result of vaccine damage and those whose disability occurred because they were not vaccinated'. Equating those who had taken part in Government-promoted health schemes resulting in vaccine damage with those who had refused vaccination and had been damaged by disease as a result was one of the most insensitive comments in the letter. It illustrated a total lack of understanding of the moral argument involved.

I then turned to Dr Vaughan who had offered his support while in Opposition and who had said in a letter to an Association member that Mrs Thatcher had told him she personally felt that compensation of some kind should be paid. He invited us to meet him, so Rene and I went to his office. On the way in we were met by the civil servant with whom I had the argument about the offer of £5000 and he was most upset about the meeting. I couldn't hear exactly what was being said but it was clear that he was telling Dr Vaughan that we should not be there and that the meeting should not take place. Dr Vaughan ignored him and we went into his office. We went over all the old arguments but again without result. Whatever he had said in the past would have no influence on Government policy now, he said, and our meeting ended in disappointment.

It is difficult to explain the sense of betrayal I felt when he said this. The spokesman appointed by Margaret Thatcher had gone out of his way to be helpful and to express support for our campaign with her approval. Dr Vaughan was the appointed spokesman during all the debates, not Patrick Jenkin, and yet here we were with the latter in the position of power and the former obviously unable to insist on living up to his promises.

As in the 1970s, I looked around for ways in which the situation could be altered. After the initial relief which the £10,000 payment provided for parents, there was anger at the amount which contrasted with compensation sums being paid in Court for much lesser injuries.

I wrote to Lord Pearson to ask for his comments on the contrast between the payment and his recommendation for strict liability, and he replied with a three-page handwritten statement.

While saying that he adhered to the recommendations in the Royal Commission report, he went on to say that 'in view of the present state, and the prospects for the near future, of British Industry and the national economy, the general strategy of the Government is naturally to cut down public expenditure', and he could not conscientiously contend that further public funds should be made available at the present time.

Those Members of Parliament to whom I continued to write said that cuts in pensions and services for the elderly and disabled were being made in Parliament every week and MPs were powerless to do anything about it. Jack Ashley was now free to campaign again and he also advised that it would be at least a year, if not much more, before there was any point in promoting our cause again in the House.

Finally, I decided to write to the Prime Minister, Margaret Thatcher. To begin with, I kept receiving non-committal replies from her office, so I sent her a personal letter to say that I was never sure whether she saw my letters and please could she reply herself. This brought a personal reply from Mrs Thatcher on 4 January 1982. She did not mention vaccine damage or her previously reported support. She simply repeated that Government policy was to improve provision for all disabled people generally, which compounded the sense of betrayal that I felt.

In February 1982, I wrote to Association members to report the position about any future campaign. Following my meeting with Dr Vaughan, I had also gone to the House of Commons to talk to David Ennals, and to Jack Ashley, now a member of the Oppostion, to ask for their opinion about carrying on the campaign at that time. They both repeated what Lord Pearson had said previously that, in view of the economic position at the time, it would be at least a year, possibly two, before there would be any point in renewing a campaign for compensation.

They repeated that cuts in pensions and services for the elderly and disabled were being made in Parliament every week and there was no way in which large compensation payments could be expected.

There were many groups representing disabled people campaigning for provision at the time and, whatever the rights of vaccine-damaged children, there was little sympathy for those who wanted special provision. Margaret Thatcher had no intention of allowing any increases in public spending to upset her policy of stringent economy.

At that stage, I gave up all hope of an easy answer and started again on the long job of writing lobbying letters to MPs, keeping up publicity about our campaign, repeating our arguments about the need for a compensation scheme for vaccine damage and urging all the parents concerned to do the same.

In the circumstances, it was naïve to suggest that we would have to wait for a year or two. As things turned out, it was to be another 16 years before we had any hope of talking to the Government about compensation for vaccine damage again.

14

Marshalling the Law

When I told parents in 1982 that there was little hope of an early promise of full compensation from the Government, there were different reactions. Some said it was hopeless, that they were glad to have received £10,000 but they didn't want to carry on any further. Others said they would never give up and would now consider legal action. At the time, there were 635 families on my circulation list and I asked those who wanted to carry on to sign a confirmation slip to this effect. Approximately 320 confirmed and the rest did not reply. Much later, some of those who did not reply complained that they had heard nothing from the Association for years, but their names were always kept and available for the Vaccine Damage Payment Unit when required.

In a small organisation, funded on a very casual basis by contributions from members, it would have been impossible to keep constant contact with over 600 families, given the costs of paper, printing and postage. For the 300 letters we continued to send out, most of the costs were borne by me and those who constantly helped me through the years.

By this stage, because of all the publicity about the £10,000 payment, the number of applications to the Payment Unit had reached over 2,000. A large proportion of the claims failed, which added to the anger felt by parents. However, it was always obvious that with any compensation scheme it would be necessary to provide evidence to support a claim, and with these claims it was particularly necessary to have a vaccination record card, to show what vaccination took place on what date, and it was also necessary to say what reaction the vaccination caused, how soon after the vaccination it occurred and to which doctor or clinic it was reported. These details enabled claims to be assessed 'on the balance of probabilities' which was the standard of proof required under the Payment Act.

Merely being convinced that it was the vaccination which caused the damage to the child was not enough, but that was not a popular thing to say to parents and talking about the need to prove their claim by producing relevant medical details was sometimes taken as a lack of support. This level of proof required under the Act was of course completely different to that which would be required in Court where evidence of negligence and proof of causation would be required.

Negligence might be demonstrated if the vaccination went ahead in face of known contraindications, or if there was proof that the vaccine was faulty. Causation needed scientific evidence from experts who could demonstrate how the vaccine caused the damage once it was injected, or evidence from a scientific study which could prove the vaccine risk.

The thoughts of many parents now turned towards legal action, and there was widespread interest at the time over the first British case to be heard. Legal proceedings had been started as early as 1979, when Iris and John Bonthrone, the parents of Richard, sued the Secretary of State for Scotland, Fife Health Board, the GP who administered the triple vaccine and the health visitor attached to the doctor's practice. Their case was that Richard had suffered a reaction to his first triple vaccination, but further vaccinations were given which amounted to negligence.

The first preliminary hearing of the case was in 1981 when the claim against the Secretary of State was dismissed. The Bonthrones continued to sue the other three parties, claiming compensation of £250,000 and, after another year, the Judge, Lord Jauncey, ruled that the case could go to trial, beginning in May 1983. It had taken four years to get this far.

Days before the trial was to begin, the Health Board produced a diagnosis for the Court of the cause of

Richard's condition, claiming that he suffered from microcephaly which they said was a disorganisation of the brain's growth system. This new claim by the Board had transformed the case, the Judge said, and it would have to be put back, possibly for a year until 1984. There was much criticism of this late defence from the Health Board and an apology to the parents for yet another delay in the hearing of their case.

The case finally began in January 1985, eight years after Iris Bonthrone first went to see her solicitor. It had been agreed beforehand that, if the case was proved, the amount of damages to be awarded for Richard would be £145,000, and it was therefore particularly distressing for the family when, feeling they might be able to provide extra care for Richard from such a sum, their case failed. Six medical experts gave conflicting opinions on the cause of Richard's condition and, having analysed these, Lord Jauncey ruled that Mr and Mrs Bonthrone had not proved that the brain damage to their son was caused by whooping cough vaccine. He agreed that the whole story was an 'appalling tragedy' but it was one with which Richard's parents would have to cope without any additional resources resulting from the case.

Despite the ruling against the Bonthrone's case, there were elements in the Judge's ruling which other solicitors saw as helpful in pursuing other cases. He reached a general conclusion that, 'on very rare occasions and within appropriate time limits, pertussis (whooping cough) vaccine can cause severe and permanent brain damage'.

One such other solicitor was Jack Rabinowicz of Teacher Stern Selby in London, who, at the time, was instructed in the case of Susan Loveday, which was to provide further rulings on the whole issue when it came to the High Court in London in 1987.

During the delays in the Scottish case, the first English case came to the High Court in London. In 1980, Michael Kinnear, the father of Johnnie, successfully claimed the £10,000 vaccine damage payment but, feeling that this was inadequate, and aided by a very sympathetic solicitor, he sued the Health Authority, the Department of Health and Social Security and the manufacturer of the vaccine, the Wellcome Foundation. The DHSS tried in the High Court to have the case against it dismissed, but failed, although it turned out that Kinnear could not proceed because of a lack of funds. Having allowed up to £250,000 of legal aid to be spent on the preparation of the case, the Law Society refused any further funds

Following an appeal, the Law Society agreed to restore legal aid but only for actions against the doctor and health authority, meaning that actions against the DHSS and Wellcome could not proceed. Wellcome, on the other hand, were given leave to assist the Judge when the case came to court, arguing that it had already undertaken considerable preparation for the case, that it had unique expertise, that it could assist the Judge in reaching his decision and that it was in the public interest to do so, adding that it would pay its own costs whatever the outcome of the case. So a situation was created in which

129

the manufacturer could argue in support of its product, without any restrictions on the cost of its involvement in the case, while the Kinnears would not be able to pursue the manufacturer for damages.

The hearing in the case before Mr Justice Stuart-Smith began in February 1986 but, to quote the *New Scientist Report* of 26 February 1987, it was 'a test case that died in infancy'. Several weeks into the trial, the Queen's Counsel representing the Kinnear family said he could not go on with the case as it was not possible to corroborate the parents' testimony regarding Johnnie's condition when he was vaccinated.

The Loveday case followed on the heels of the Kinnear case and related to the case of Susan Loveday, who had been vaccinated as a baby and had reportedly suffered a severe reaction to the whooping cough vaccine included in the triple. Applications under the Vaccine Damage Payment Act of 1979 had been unsuccessful, as had appeals to the Vaccine Damage Tribunal, as the criteria for establishing a successful claim on the balance of probabilities had not been met.

Her case was one of those put down for hearing following the Kinnear case and, in line with established procedure, the Court called her case as the next to be heard in the High Court of Justice, Queen's Bench Division, before The Rt Hon Lord Justice Stuart-Smith. The trial took 4 months, 19 expert witnesses gave evidence and the Judgment, which ran to over 100,000 words, and took 2 days to read, was given on 29 and 30 March 1988.

Because of the result of the Kinnear trial, when, after a great deal of time and expense, the hearing was stopped because of conflicting evidence from the parents about the events surrounding the vaccination, the Judge in the Loveday case decided that the case would be split. He would first of all concentrate on just one issue – 'Can whooping cough vaccine cause brain damage.' If the answer to that was 'yes', he would then go on to consider the details of the vaccination and the issue of whether there had been negligence by the doctor being sued.

At the end of the long trial, the very detailed expert discussions about the vaccine and its possible role in causing brain damage, and a particularly detailed analysis of the most recent study into the whole question of whooping cough vaccine damage – *The National Childhood Encephalopathy Study* – the Judge ruled:

'I have now come to the clear conclusion that the Plaintiff fails to satisfy me on the balance of probability that pertussis vaccine can cause permanent brain damage in young children. It is possible that it does; the contrary cannot be proved. But in the result, the Plaintiff's claim must fail.'

The Judgement was hailed by all the medical proponents of whooping cough vaccination, who had previously and subsequently referred to the campaign for vaccine-damaged children as a 'scare'. They concentrated concern on what they called a vast increase in the number of children who got whooping cough as a result of bad publicity and the large numbers who died.

From then on, it was noticeable that all those most violently opposed to any criticism of whooping cough vaccine became selective about the Judge's ruling and were prepared to quote only the first sentence – 'The plaintiff fails to satisfy me on the balance of probability that pertussis vaccine can cause permanent damage in young children.' They carefully avoided any mention of the qualification 'it is possible that it does; the contrary cannot be proved...' which to any unbiased person has to mean that the whole question is still an open one.

The strength of feeling from the medical critics was perhaps best summed up in a *Lancet* article on 17 February 1990. 'The High Court,' it reported, 'has vindicated the vaccine entirely and suggested that, far from causing encephalopathy, it probably protects against it.' The author thanked the Wellcome Foundation 'for their tenacity in defending their vaccine' and then went on to suggest five steps the Government should take to rectify its national policy, the first of which was that the Vaccine Damage Payment Act of 1979 should be repealed, and the last of which was that the advice about whooping cough vaccination contained in the Department of Health handbook should be modified to omit any reference to vaccine damage.

Even today, 15 years later, there are health specialists who continue to say that the campaign for vaccine-damaged children led to three epidemics of the disease in the 1970s, during which 'hundreds of thousands of children got whooping cough and more than 100 children died as a result'. As an example of a gross misrepresentation of the actual figures, it takes some beating, and although I have written to one of the specialists concerned asking for a correction, the misrepresentation continues. The true figures are included in an official Department of Health report entitled *Whooping Cough* which was published in May 1981.

Section VI of the Report covered 'The Whooping Cough Epidemic 1977 - 79'.

'In 1974,' the report began, 'after reports appeared in the media of brain damage alleged to have been caused in children by whooping cough vaccination, the acceptance levels for vaccine by children in England fell'

The report went on to say that, as a consequence, the next epidemic of the disease, expected at a periodicity of 3 to 4 years, would be at least as great and possibly greater than the preceding one of 1974-75. 'The epidemic became apparent in the last quarter of 1977 and can be considered to have subsided by mid 1979 during which time 102,500 cases were notified in the United Kingdom.' The report said this was higher than for any similar period since the vaccine was introduced.

From the beginning of the epidemic to the end of 1980, 28 deaths were notified.

'This number is smaller than would have been expected from the case fatality ratios in previous outbreaks' the report went on, but considering that the actual number of deaths was not fully reflected in the notifications for the UK, 5 deaths from whooping cough and 3 in Northern Ireland were added – making a total of 36.

Despite these official figures, there are still doctors critical of our campaign who continue at every opportunity to say that it led to 3 epidemics, during which 'hundreds of thousands of children got whooping cough and more than 100 died as a result.' A year-by-year analysis of the true figures would not support such statements. Despite these official figures, there are still doctors who were critical of our campaign and who continue at every opportunity to say that it led to three epidemics during which hundreds of thousands of children got whooping cough and more than 100 died as a result. A year-by-year analysis of the true figures would not support such statements.

The Vaccine Damage Payment Act covered all vaccines – from smallpox vaccine which had been withdrawn in 1972 to diphtheria, tetanus, whooping cough, measles, oral polio and inactivated polio, rubella, BCG – which had caused severe reactions that had resulted in damage. Repealing such an Act because of one disputed vaccine could hardly be seen as a reasonable act. As regards the Department of Health handbook, it had, from 1962, when the first booklet was issued to doctors, referred to the possibility of reaction to whooping cough vaccination and pointed out conditions in which use of the vaccine would be inadvisable. Wellcome themselves had included a leaflet with their earlier doses of vaccine warning of the importance of allergies in relation to vaccination with whooping cough vaccine, so it could hardly be suddenly pretended that there was no need for guidance.

The failure of the Loveday case provided ammunition for those in the medical profession who wanted to direct criticism at the Association of Parents and our campaign for compensation for vaccine-damaged children. Later, however, it was also to be used by a few of the parents themselves who, despite all the evidence to the contrary, were determined to say that it was the fact that the Loveday case was seen as a test case which created difficulties for everyone in pursuing a claim for their own child, because the Loveday claim under the Vaccine Damage Payment Act had not succeeded.

No matter how often it was said that it was the Court which listed the next claim to be heard after the Kinnear case, these parents would not be convinced. Neither would they accept that the result would have been the same whatever case had gone forward as a test case. The trial was not concerned with the details of the vaccination itself or the nature of the reaction, but with the expert arguments about whether and how whooping cough vaccination caused the damage and the Judge's ruling dealt with these arguments and nothing else.

A few years later, for some parents, all the upset and feelings of powerlessness and abandonment surfaced, resulting in a split in the Association.

Naturally, all the parents were very disappointed with the result of the trial. It had been ten years since they had received the £10,000 payment and it was clear to everyone that, as long as a Conservative Government was in office, there would be no further provision. Everyone had seen the case as a possible way forward to pusuing their own legal actions, so that they could begin to plan for the future care of their children, many of whom were now young adults needing special help to enable them to live with dignity either at home or in care.

On 31 March 1988, all the Association families were informed of the very disappointing Judgment and told that the acting solicitors hoped to know in a month or so whether an Appeal against the Judgment would be made. The Judgment referred only to whooping cough vaccine, of course, and there were other vaccines covered by the Payment Act.

Although I promised to try to arrange meetings with solicitors involved with the other vaccines, this was never an easy task. All of the publicity and the legal action to date had been about whooping cough vaccine and it was considered by all that a breakthrough on a whooping cough case would ease the way for other cases. It was probably for this reason that there was no action taken by solicitors who had been approached about vaccines such as measles, rubella, polio or smallpox. This is still the case to the present day. It was also true that the parents of cases such as these did not take an active role in the appointment of solicitors or in discussions about legal action. They, too, had heard nothing but talk about whooping cough vaccine and many felt they were being ignored.

The decision of the Legal Aid Board was not to fund an Appeal against the Loveday Judgment, but the Board had previously told Jack Ashley that 'If there were an effective vaccine damage action group with a co-ordinating group of solicitors conducting the cases, then it might be possible for the Court and Legal Aid to support a lead group of cases to test the causation issue.' With this advice in mind, a meeting of parents and their solicitors was called for September 1988 at The Victory Services Club.

This meeting resulted in the setting up of a Steering Committee of Solicitors, chaired by Jack Rabinowicz, who spent the next eight years working to find a way of pursuing successful legal action on behalf of all the parents who had voted them in and who were prepared to support their efforts.

The Committee comprised Jack Rabinowicz, Teacher Stern Selby, London (Chairman); Elizabeth Thompson, David & Snape, Bridgend; Clare Harper, Kidd & Spoor, Newcastle-upon-Tyne; Graham Ross, J Keith Park and Co, St Helens; Denise Airey, Wren Hilton Apfel, Lytham St Annes; Maurice Nichols, AE Wyeth & Co, Dartford; and Claire Horton, Linder Myers, Manchester.

The meeting also resulted in an offer from one of the parents present to take over some of the work of preparing and distributing circular letters to other parents. This was Sheila Casson, a Magistrate who had a secretarial business and had the printing facilities we needed. Sheila's daughter, Vicki, was vaccine damaged and Sheila's husband John took a large share of the work of looking after her. This eased my workload considerably and it became even better when another parent, John Cheesman, who had access to a typing agency agreed to split the work with Sheila and take on circulation to the parents in the South. Both of these parents attended meetings with MPs and Government officials and Sheila became a lay member of the Steering Committee.

Helen was now 25 and her specialists were suggesting that we needed to be thinking of her future care. David and I were in our sixties and, although we felt that we would be able to care for Helen forever, staying at home with us was not exactly interesting and stimulating for her. Also, during my time at social services, I had come across cases where elderly parents died and their disabled children, who had continued to live with them, had to be taken into care homes and looked after by people who were strangers to them. We did not want that to happen to Helen. She started staying in a local residential care home at weekends and after a period of about 2 years she moved in on a permanent basis.

It was a sad day for us and it took a few years before we could finally accept that this was the best arrangement for Helen and that she was happy. She had the company of four other residents and the care and attention of a large, highly committed staff. From then on I had more freedom to travel and more time to sit at my typewriter to keep our arguments going.

To begin with, the Steering Committee's aim was to seek reinstatement of legal aid. Following the Judgment, the Deputy Director of the Legal Aid Board Area 8 Office had discharged all but four of the legal aid certificates and also refused all pending and proposed applications for legal aid. A number of appeals against the Legal Aid Board decision were lodged and seven of the unsuccessful applicants sought Judicial Review of the Board's decision. The Review was successful and, in March 1990, Justice Simon Brown ordered that the Legal Aid Committee's decision should be quashed and the appeals should be reheard by a differently constituted Legal Aid Committee.

In preparation for this new hearing, another meeting of parents was called for 11 May 1990 to bring them up to date with the legal aid position and to encourage them to inform the solicitors acting on their behalf about the new appeal. Following that meeting, the Chairman of the Steering Committee, Jack Rabinowicz , was able to write to the solicitors representing the parents seeking information about their cases in preparation for the Appeal hearing. Mr Rupert Jackson QC was instructed in relation to the Appeal hearing which took place on 24 and 25 January 1991, at which 87 applicants were successfully represented by the Steering Committee. There then followed long and difficult discussions with the Legal Aid Board. Jack

Rabinowicz wanted legal aid granted in all cases so that every applicant could obtain medical notes and records, which could then be vetted by a medical expert and referred to Counsel for an Opinion. The Board rejected this proposal and parents were then asked to instruct their own solicitors to lobby the Legal Aid Board to support the Steering Committee's proposal that limited legal aid should be given to at least carry out some initial investigations.

By November 1991, 135 solicitors had contacted the Steering Committee on behalf of their clients and, for the next few months, both Jack Rabinowicz as Chair of the Steering Committee and I as Association Secretary were kept busier than usual arranging the collection of information from parents in order to compile a database, as well as talking to the medical experts involved and researching for expert reports. Eventually, in March 1992, it was possible to have a meeting with three of the recommended medical experts – Dr Newton, Dr Brett and Dr Wilson.

They discussed the current position with regards to research and understanding of vaccine damage and they outlined the kind of documentation which would be required to enable them to report back on cases referred to them. All of this information was passed on to the solicitors on the Steering Committee's mailing list to ensure that they would be able to provide the experts with detailed and constructive information.

At a Steering Committee meeting which took place in December 1992, I reported that some parents were complaining about the lack of feedback from their solicitors, which I found surprising in view of the detailed information going out to the solicitors from the Committee. The Committee Chairman then reported that he also was surprised at the lack of contact from the solicitors, and it was agreed that, to avoid any misunderstandings, Jack Rabinowicz would send out bulletins to all the solicitors on his list as and when there was important news. Several bulletins subsequently went out to all the relevant solicitors to keep them fully updated as to the latest developments.

All of these bulletins were records of all of the work done by the Steering Committee over an eight-year period in an attempt to bring another case to Court on behalf of those damaged by whooping cough vaccine. The record shows the constant struggle with the Legal Aid Board for funds to carry out the necessary work, the meetings arranged with experts to get advice about the preparation of cases, the journeys undertaken by Committee members to attend meetings, gather information, argue legal points, prepare instructions and meet with Counsel, and the constant research both here and abroad in order to prepare an effective case. All of the work was hampered by the constant struggle with the Legal Aid Board over inadequate funding and, in fact, a considerable portion of the time spent, and the delay in approaching Counsel, was due to this contest.

Members of the Committee spent what amounted to thousands of hours of chargeable time attempting to progress the litigation, almost all of which was unfunded. Over the five-year period, keeping all the solicitors who had registered an interest in the litigation informed involved thousands of letters.

Following the issue of Bulletin No. 8 in March 1995, regarding the choice of Leading Counsel to advise on a further Court case, Mr Daniel Brennan QC, recognised as one of the leading personal injury Silks in the country, was approached and, after meetings with the Steering Committee and a six-hour conference with medical experts – Dr Wilson, Professor Behan and Professor Menkes from the United States – Mr Brennan accepted the Instruction to prepare an Advice. The Advice was provided in December 1996 and was the subject of Bulletin No. 9 to solicitors from the Steering Committee in March 1997 and a letter from me calling a meeting of parents on 1 June 1997 at the Victory Services Club, Seymour Street.

The meeting was called to report on the present position regarding legal action, to give parents details of Counsel's Opinion and also to report on the position regarding the campaign during the years while further legal action was being investigated, something which was particularly important in view of the recent election of a Labour Government.

15

Staying Power

During the eight years after the Loveday Judgment, while the Steering Committee laboured constantly to regain the legal aid which had been withdrawn, to improve it in the hope of proceeding with new cases, and to carry out extensive research in order to be prepared to instruct the QC, the parliamentary campaign for the children continued unabated.

Patrick Jenkin, as the incoming Secretary of State in 1979, had said with a great lack of sensitivity that he was concerned as much for those damaged by disease because they had not been vaccinated as he was for those damaged by vaccination. Mrs Thatcher had followed this up in 1982 with the statement that she could see no significant discrepancy between her Opposition policy and her present policy of improving provision for the disabled generally – this despite her appointment of Dr Vaughan as a spokesman in Opposition who said there should be compensation for vaccine damage.

There were many times in the face of such a completely negative attitude to the principles which we were addressing that I felt like giving up and, indeed, in the early 1990s, particularly after the Loveday Judgment, there were many parents who said they felt it was all a waste of time and stopped their constant contact with the Association. Although the names of all the original 630 family contacts remained on our database, the number of constant contacts fell to just under 300, but these were the determined parents who attended meetings, corresponded with their Members of Parliament and took every opportunity available to talk about their damaged children to the press or television.

My parliamentary campaign file bulges with copies of Early Day Motions, Parliamentary Questions and Debates in the Commons and the Lords from 1980 to 1997; many of those taking part are now household names, such as Kenneth Clarke, who was Secretary of State for Health, and Lord Henley, Under-Secretary of State for Health.

Jack Ashley had lost no time in raising the question of compensation with the new administration and put down many Early Day Motions deploring the Government's refusal to establish a compensation scheme and calling for an urgent review of the Vaccine Damage Payments Scheme.

These were followed later by a debate in the House of Lords by Lord Campbell of Alloway and, from then on, there was a succession of similar Motions and Debates, many of which resulted in helpful press and television publicity.

There was an interesting controversy surrounding one *World in Action* programme in 1982 when the researcher, looking through my files to gather details for her programme, came across a letter from Kenneth Clark, written when in Opposition in 1975, stating that he had signed an Early Day Motion supporting our call for compensation. As Mr Clark was now Secretary of State for Social Services, the researcher, who had arranged an interview with him as part of the programme, said she would ask him about his letter during the interview. I could see nothing wrong with that and would possibly have asked him about it myself during subsequent campaigning.

However, the manner in which the letter was presented to him caused Mr Clark much annoyance; having asked him if he agreed to compensation for vaccine damage, to which he said 'no', as it was not Government policy, the researcher then produced his letter, which seemed to show, at the very least, a change of heart.

Watching the programme, even though I thought it was a bit unfair I felt that it was entirely a matter for the programme director.

When a member of the Association wrote to Margaret Thatcher to criticise Mr Clarke's appearance on the *World in Action* programme, it was obvious from the very irate reply from Chris Butler of the Political Office at No. 10 Downing Street that Mr Clark was furious and that his fury was shared by others in the Cabinet. Accusing the programme producers of trickery and unfair editing, Mr Butler went on to criticise me personally: 'Mrs Fox is unfortunately now claiming that every expression of sympathy that anybody gave to her before 1979 somehow was an endorsement of her present claim that hundreds of thousands of pounds should be paid to each of these children in a full scheme of compensation.'

I was surprised at the vehemence of the attack and also annoyed because what he said was untrue. Far from suggesting large compensation payments for each child, I had been suggesting, as one option, that the Department should consider a severe disability pension from age 16, similar to War Pensions, which at the time was about £54 per week. This was the way provision for severe vaccine damage was dealt with in Germany, one of the European countries to have such a scheme at the time.

I wrote to Mr Butler to say if he could find any evidence in any of my literature which suggested that I was seeking 'hundreds of thousands of pounds per child', I would be glad if he would send me a copy, or otherwise withdraw his statement. I also pointed out to him that everything Ministers had said to me about the campaign was a matter of record, and that all I had done was show the letters to the programme researcher to support what was being said – i.e. that in Opposition there were many statements of support for the claim for compensation.

Mr Butler eventually wrote to say that both he and Mr Clarke accepted that my two corrections of his letter were valid and that they would be more careful in future.

Fortunately, there was no repetition of this in any of the Association's future publicity. In so far as I had any say in the matter, I made sure it did not happen again.

The Early Day Motions, debates and media articles carried on hopefully for the next eight years, with a lot of encouragement from Members of Parliament and others who could see the justice of our claim, but with little sign of success. In 1990, we were all encouraged by a Debate in the House by a Conservative Member of Parliament, Alistair Burt, speaking on behalf of his constituent, Bernice. To have a Conservative MP campaigning was quite a significant event, and when he wrote to me for details I went to a lot of trouble to make sure that Alistair Burt had all the details he would need to ensure that his debate was significant.

He spoke to the House of Commons on 27 June 1990. This was a late debate which started at 1.10am, and it was a measure of the concern felt by Alistair Burt and by the MPs who later joined him in the debate – Ken Hargreaves, MP for Hyndburn, and Anthony Coombs, MP for Wyre Forest, that they waited in the Chamber until that hour to plead our cause. Surely, we thought, the Conservative Government will listen to one of its own Members of Parliament and finally take part in some discussions about our children. Alistair Burt was very sincere in his desire to help vaccine-damaged children and had worked hard to bring their claim to the attention of his own Government.

Alistair Burt started his speech by arguing the case for a larger capital award and a review of the 80% disability rule. He suggested that the pharmaceutical companies should be asked to support a fund and, in closing, he recorded the fact that concern about the Vaccine Damage Payment Act had been widespread for many years and he suggested to the Government that the time had come to look at the matter again.

Stephen Dorrell, Parliamentary Under-Secretary of State for Health, replied for the Government. He spent six minutes talking about immunisation in general, about the improved uptake and the decrease in disease as a result. He gave detailed statistics about whooping cough cases and then gave a description of the Vaccine Damage Payment Act and what it was intended to do. Since it was clear from the outset that he had only a limited time in which to respond, it appeared that he was talking out the debate so as to avoid a direct answer to Alistair Burt's request. In fact, all he managed to say before the Speaker adjourned the House was that the technical details of the Payment Act were matters for the Department of Social Security.

Unfortunately, the response was, as usual, 'it is Government policy to help all disabled children', so the campaign had to carry on.

So again we returned to lobbying MPs and looking again at the possibility of legal action in order to get provision for our damaged children. One answer always given by the Government when refusing to look at the

Payment Act was that, of course, we always had the right to seek compensation in the Courts, but they said this knowing full well that legal action was far from easy. To begin with, without proof of negligence there was no basis for the action, and even if this hurdle was cleared, there remained the need to prove causation.

There was a breakthrough in 1993 when Margaret Best successfully sued Wellcome in the Irish Courts, having been able to show that the batch of vaccine which was used for the vaccination of her son, Kenneth, had not been properly tested. The award in the Dublin High Court, which was for £2.75 million pounds, was greeted with delight by parents hoping to take their cases to the High Court in London, and it not only gave fresh impetus to the search for a way ahead through legal action here but it also provided publicity, which highlighted the poor comparison between what the Government was prepared to do for those who had suffered and what the Court felt was necessary to provide lifelong care.

The publicity resulting from Margaret's success revived our campaign and, to begin with, I wrote to our parents in November 1993 stressing the need to involve their MPs. So that a detailed report could go out, I asked parents to write to me or telephone with the name of their MP so that I could write on their behalf.

In the New Year, I was able to tell them that I had some very interesting replies from some of the 140 MPs and Ministers to whom I had written, and who had sent on my letter to the Department of Health. The Department of Health then sent the letters to the DHSS, and the official reply from that department was, as usual, that the Government's aim was to help all disabled people, irrespective of the cause of their disability.

I also constantly referred the matter to John Major, the Prime Minister, who sent brief acknowledgments via his secretaries, or referred the matter to the DHSS for reply and, in 1994, when William Hague was the Minister for Social Security and Disabled People, I also wrote to him. What I got back by way of reply was a short note restating the Conservative position, pinned to the original of a letter I had sent previously to John Major, which was now rather crumpled, and I was again reminded of the insensitivity which some individuals in that particular Government could display in their dealings with people. I was annoyed at what I saw to be a dismissive gesture, and I wanted to say that if they couldn't find a file to put my letter in, then they could put it in the bin. What I did write was that sending me back my letter in that way was very poor practice and one I had never previously come across from any of the Ministers I had written to over the years.

It was the first time I had become aware of the difference in approach between Conservative and Labour Ministers. The former continued to be distant and unfriendly and left it to their secretaries and advisers to reply and to sign letters. Labour Ministers, on the other hand, were always prepared to offer meetings, send personal responses and maintain friendly contact.

When I referred the question of proper provision for vaccine damage directly to William Hague as Minister for Disabled People, his reply followed the long-established Conservative pattern. The Government's position on the scheme, he said, is that it operates in a fair and effective manner – 'a view which I share'. He was later to write to the newly elected Labour administration supporting their decision to amend the Payment Act and improve the Payment.

By now, Jack Ashley, as The Right Hon Lord Ashley of Stoke, was campaigning for vaccine-damaged children in the House of Lords and keeping close contact with responsible Ministers. It was also a great relief to again have a Member of the House of Commons dedicated to the work of keeping the campaign alive in Parliament.

Following a letter lobby of MPs arranged in 1993, Richard Burden MP for Northfield, Birmingham, wrote to say he was interested in pursuing a campaign in Parliament on the subject. Together with some of my colleagues, I went to the House of Commons to meet Richard in February 1994 and passed on to him various notes about the campaign, together with a list of the Members of Parliament who had written following the lobby letter to say they would be happy to support any further action.

On 23 May 1994, Richard put down Early Day Motion No. 1271 calling for an amendment to the Vaccine Damage Payment Act to remove the six-year limit on the period in which claims could be made, to cover all degrees of disability and to increase the provision under the Act. The Motion received immediate support from MPs from all parts of the House and, within the first two days, had 142 signatures, some from MPs who became Ministers of State in the next Government. By the end of July, the total number of signatures was 199 and Richard arranged for a press conference to take place at 7 Millbank. This was attended by supporting MPs and parents' representatives who attended with me, included Sheila Casson, the Association's Northern Secretary; Jackie Fletcher and Ann Coote of the Justice, Awareness and Basic Support (JABS) group; and a parent whose son had suffered from polio vaccination.

We were beginning to feel that in the face of the Government's reluctance to accept any responsibility and their constant reference to the impossibility of proving vaccine damage that it was time to introduce another argument. The campaign for compensation had always been based on whooping cough vaccination as this was the one which had created most anxiety among medical experts and was obviously responsible for most of the cases of vaccine damage we were dealing with, but there were also cases of severe reaction to polio vaccination which were seldom mentioned, and in these cases causation was easier to demonstrate. The time had come, we felt, to be a bit more open about vaccination details which the Department of Health would prefer not to have mentioned, but which could have a more dramatic effect on our arguments about Government responsibility.

Oral polio vaccine had been introduced in 1962 and had successfully wiped out natural polio in the following years. It was only when the natural disease had been eliminated, however, that the cases of disease from the vaccine became obvious and, by 1994, there were worrying statistics about such cases. Figures from the Department of Health showed that there were at least 37 cases of polio during the years 1987 to 1992, a few of which were imported but most of which resulted from the vaccination. The Department also confirmed that one or two cases of polio resulted from one million doses of the vaccine. In the Early Day Motion, we had referred to 'cases of partial paralysis from polio vaccination excluded from the Payment Act because of the 80% disability rule', and we were now prepared to talk openly about this vaccine.

In the event, there wasn't a press conference because there was a BBC strike and there were many other press conferences taking place about the European elections being held at the time. The summer recess was just starting and, as I wrote to parents, our job during the months ahead was to keep in constant touch with our MPs and keep Richard Burden's campaign successfully supported. As before, I wrote to MPs on behalf of parents and also sent a prepared postcard to parents to send on themselves.

In the following months, Richard Burden put down a steady stream of Parliamentary Questions to elicit information about the Government's handling of vaccination policies and their attitude to the Vaccine Damage Payment. In April 1996, following another well supported Early Day Motion, he introduced a Bill in Parliament aimed at improving compensation for children damaged by mass immunisation programmes. This was a Ten-Minute Rule Bill which, although seldom resulting in legislation, provides a unique opportunity to debate particular subjects and, on this occasion, the debate was televised, and reached a wide audience.

We were also heartened by the news that Alistair Burt, who had himself held a debate about vaccine-damaged children six years previously, was now the Minister for Social Security and Disabled People and, following Richard's debate and the Early Day Motion, we both felt it would be a good time to write to Alistair Burt asking for a meeting. This took place on 19 November 1996 and was attended by Richard Burden MP, Jackie Fletcher of JABS and myself, but although we had a courteous reception and a detailed response from Alistair Burt, it again resulted in a refusal to consider further provision.

Without Richard Burden's constant interest and involvement in keeping the case before Parliament (particularly in the period before the election which returned a Labour Government) it would not have been so easy to bring it up straight away after the election. I went up and down to see him to bring files and case details and help with the preparation of Early Day Motions. But he didn't say how his interest in the matter had arisen and I assumed that he was one of the Members of Parliament who recognised injustice when he saw it and worked to put things right. He did have two constituents with vaccine damaged children but I didn't know anything about that until later.

We were now approaching another election which, as usual, held up progress. I don't know if other campaigners find the same thing, but I always found it ironic that every time we seemed to be on the verge of success, an election or Parliamentary scandal or an uprising abroad or a fire or flood at home would occur just in time to draw attention away from our cause.

However, we hoped that the election would produce a Labour Government which would not only be sympathetic to our cause, but which could also be challenged to honour the statement made by David Ennals in 1979 that the £10,000 payment was 'not the end'.

When the election produced a Labour Government, a meeting of parents was called to discuss the two courses of action – initially to take full advantage of the opportunity to go back to a Labour Government to get them to honour the Ennals' statement, and also to consider legal action in the light of the most recent Counsel's Opinion.

The meeting was held at the Victory Services Club on 1 June 1997 but, far from providing an opportunity to co-ordinate the work for the benefit of the parents, it was to be the cause of splitting up the parents' campaign and breaking up the work of the solicitors' legal action committee. We had come such a long way, achieving some significant successes, and had supported each other through so many dispiriting times as well, so it was heartbreaking to see the Association being fragmented and undermined when there was still so much to gain. Some were not convinced of the Association's methods, but for those of us that were, the fight had to go on.

16

Dissent into Chaos

I will never forget or forgive what took place at the meeting on 1 June 1997. To begin with, I wanted parents to have details of the latest Advice from Daniel Brennan QC and to know what was being proposed as the best way to proceed with litigation. After that, I wanted to discuss the need to run another vigorous parliamentary campaign now that a Labour Government had returned to power. We now had the opportunity to request that they honour the promise made in 1979 that the Vaccine Damage Payment was not the end. Not only that, but we could now confidently carry on with our campaign in view of a recent statement from Frank Field, Minister of State for Welfare Reform, that the Government fully recognised the long-standing concerns about vaccine-damage payments and would examine the

Vaccine Damage Payment Scheme critically in the light of those concerns.

This was a very definite statement of intent to review the whole payment arrangements and, to my mind, our next step was to keep pressing for the review with the help of all the Members of Parliament who had promised us support.

Sadly, it was not to Frank Field himself that we would be able to address our claims, as he left his office shortly afterwards, but I have always thought that, without his statement at the time, our task would have been very much harder over the following three years.

As for the litigation, Daniel Brennan QC had advised that he saw no reasonable prospects of justifying further action in respect of the conventional claims, but he did see a case for investigating 'defective batch' claims like that of Kenneth Best in Ireland, whose legal action had been successful, and it was Mr Brennan's opinion that this was the type of case which would stand a better chance of success.

Letters had gone to all Association parents asking them to attend. Solicitors were not invited, as the Steering Committee had decided to arrange such a meeting later.

Before the meeting, there were some rumblings of discontent from some of the parents who were aware of the Brennan Advice. This was not altogether surprising since so many were relying on Court action to gain proper compensation for the damage to their own children.

Allied to the disappointment about Counsel's Opinion

was disappointment about the lack of any firm Government proposals, despite the continuing campaign, and a handful of parents decided that this was all the fault of the Steering Committee and myself. In the week before the meeting, I was told there would be a move to set up a new Association Committee and there was gossip about the intention to remove me from my role as Association Secretary and to relegate me to an honorary position as President.

The night before the meeting, I had a phone call to say the meeting would be 'hijacked' by one or two dissatisfied parents, but I didn't take much notice because I knew that most of the families with whom I had been in contact for over 20 years were sensible, reasonable people who understood that I had worked non-stop to promote our campaign and that the Steering Committee had acted faithfully on their behalf.

We had all tried hard but failed to get the Conservative Government to change its policy and acknowledge it had a special debt to vaccine-damaged children, and regular newsletters had gone out to keep everyone informed about this. Since we were not able to sue the Government for compensation, all we had to rely on was constant argument and pressure from Parliament and this we had continued to provide for all the years from 1980 onwards. The record of the work done by the Steering Committee, details of which had been sent regularly to solicitors acting for parents, spoke for itself.

My first surprise at the meeting was to see people who

had not been invited. It is an unfortunate part of meetings, which has always surprised me, that people who hear of them and feel they have some interest will attend without invitation. My disappointment was to see that there were so few Association parents present and, of course, when decisions were to be taken on the kind of important issues the Steering Committee solicitors wished to raise, it was essential that a large proportion, if not indeed all, of those involved should be there to voice their concerns or vote on issues, as had been the case at previous meetings.

After my brief opening speech to outline the meeting agenda, Jack Rabinowicz as Steering Committee Chairman, and Patrick Rafferty as Steering Committee member, addressed the meeting to explain the Brennan conclusion, talk about the kind of cases which might be able to proceed and talk again about the great difficulty of getting around the question of establishing causation, which was the main obstacle to successful legal action, an obstacle which only medical expert research could overcome. They pointed out that, to date, medical experts had not produced the kind of scientific proof of causation which a Court would need before there would be a verdict of vaccine damage. In the circumstances, they said, the way forward could be cases like Margaret Best's, where it could be shown that the vaccine used was faulty and, therefore, there could be a case based on negligence. They never got a chance to develop their argument because at that point they paused to allow questions from the floor.

The first questioner was the mother of a vaccine-damaged daughter. Initially, she spoke at length about vaccination in general terms, about how parents are pressured into vaccinating their children, about decisions taken by vaccine manufacturers in the 1970s which might suggest they were concerned about their products, about safer vaccines and about the vaccine-damage payments.

However, she then launched into a long and critical discussion about the Steering Committee, suggesting that the meeting was taking place to discuss with the Committee's solicitors the way in which they had conducted themselves over the whole pertussis vaccine damage claim. Did they know the meaning of the word 'liaise', she asked. Those who had legal aid certificates had been given an added condition to liaise with the Steering Committee and its lead case, she said, but this had not happened. What right did the Committee have, she went on, to instruct Counsel and then accept his decision, which meant throwing out most of the cases. She continued with a lot of similarly ill-informed criticism about the selection of the Loveday case, the behaviour of the Judge in that case, and the selection of consultants who were giving unfavourable reports on the cases referred. To be disappointed at the conclusions all of these lawyers had reached was understandable, but she had no medical, legal or other expert knowledge to support any of her criticisms.

She concluded that the Steering Committee and its advisers had failed the parents and she called for a motion of no confidence in the Committee. She then went on to criticise me obliquely, by saying that 'the Association is not just one particular person' and that all parents needed to be involved. She believed that the quiet approach had not been working and that parents should be 'shouting from the rooftops'.

She had been on the Association's list for a number of years but this was the first time she had attended any of our meetings or made any helpful suggestions about the campaign. There were one or two parents in the hall who obviously supported her views but did not make any statements.

I wasn't too surprised at the criticism of me because I was well aware of the minority view that the Association should have had a structured Committee, with a Chairman, a Vice-Chairman, a Treasurer, a number of committee members and possibly someone with a legal background, plus others to present a balance of views and that, in the absence of all this structure, I was being autocratic. However, the last thing I would regard as constructive is holding meetings to decide what to do and what to say, when what we were focusing on was a campaign with a single, long-established, settled argument; all that was needed was constant interest and pressure from everyone concerned to keep the argument in front of the politicians. The Association was not running a business which required overseeing, neither was it involved in any care/welfare role which would require advice, nor was it involved in collecting funds which would have made a public accountability role necessary. We were what we had always been — a group of parents acting together to press the Government to provide for our children and I believed, without undue pride, that if I had been able, together with Jack Ashley MP and the other concerned experts with whom I had established links, to get the Vaccine Damage Payment Act on the Statute Book, I could equally build on that to get a final settlement with the support and help of the parents concerned, of which 630 were listed on my database.

I was, however, stunned by the criticism of the Steering Committee and by the ignorance of the arguments put forward about the previous legal action and the Opinion from Daniel Brennan, coming as they did from someone without any professional qualifications in the fields of law or medicine. I think it showed the character and the control of the Committee that they remained in their seats and tried to answer the criticisms as politely and fully as possible.

For my part, I just looked at this parent who had been on the Association's membership list for some years, who had never before responded to any of the newsletters sent to her, who had chosen not to involve herself in the parliamentary campaign, although Richard Burden — who had been closely involved — was her MP, and who had only recently started to say she wanted to be involved and to help. To say that I was surprised is putting it mildly and, in the atmosphere created by her attitude and comments, any discussion about the campaign in parliament became impossible.

After some further questions from parents, Richard Barr, a solicitor, took the floor. He was at the time acting for a group of children said to have been damaged by the MMR [Measles, Mumps and Rubella] vaccines but also had a small number of cases of pertussis vaccine damage. He was very unhappy with the Loveday Judge who, he felt, had been much too willing to listen to the experts provided by Wellcome and felt there was a need to present the evidence to a new Judge. While expressing his sympathy with the Steering Committee, saying he had experience of being worn down over the years by the attempt to prove vaccine damage, he advised the Steering Committee to try again, noting that there were other positive Opinions from other QCs.

At the time, this seemed to be a helpful contribution. Mr Barr had not been a member of the Steering Committee as he had not represented parents who had voted in the Steering Committee members and, although Association business was not conducted on rigidly formal lines, it was nevertheless thought that as the Steering Committee had first been elected by parents and had been confirmed in that role at a subsequent meeting, the same procedure should be followed for any new member. It was also known, of course, that Mr Barr was deeply involved in the litigation concerning the Gulf War Veterans and the Sheep Dip Casualties, as well as the large MMR group.

Then a parent from the floor called for new members of the Steering Committee to be elected, saying he felt this would end the taste of acrimony which was creeping in, and those who had criticised the Steering Committee said they would be prepared to go along with them if Richard Barr was involved as well.

The meeting Chairman was Sheila Casson, a lay member of the Steering Committee, and the Northern Area Secretary of the Association. She put the question to the Meeting: 'Is a Steering Committee necessary and should one continue?' There was unanimous agreement that the Steering Committee should continue. In view of the comments which had been made, the Chairman considered that a vote to re-elect the present Steering Committee should be called but, in view of the small number of parents present, it was agreed that a postal ballot of all Association parents was needed.

To meet the implied criticism of the running of the Association campaign, I called for names to be put forward from the floor of people willing to take on a Committee role. Seven names came forward and I agreed to contact them to arrange an Association Committee meeting as soon as possible.

Although I did not know it then, the events of the day were to split the Association's campaign and the Steering Committee's legal work. As it later emerged, this was not a spontaneous occurrence at an emotional meeting but was the result of a previously formed plan by a few parents wanting to take over the Association's campaign and to reorganise the legal action under another solicitor. From that day on, the campaign was clouded by the confusion which all the criticism had created and the legal action became split between what the Steering Committee saw as the way forward, based on Counsel's Opinion at the time, and the views of another solicitor acting for another group of the parents.

Was this all my fault, I wondered. Having had close and friendly contact with hundreds of parents over the years, I never stopped to think whether they were all happy with my leadership. There had been a few mild differences of opinion about tactics but these had never developed into arguments and I could think of only three or four people who had been critical.

Was I too autocratic, I wondered. My close colleagues obviously didn't think so and we were all engaged in a fight of sorts where we had to be strong and determined. Should I invite in people who had different views about how to campaign and what to demand?

Then I thought of the 20 years that we had spent arguing our case and thought it would be a bit late in the day to change over to a new campaign. The critics at the meeting wanted to ask for very large sums of money not only as provision for their disabled children but also for the families themselves – something which would take another 20-year campaign.

I asked Sheila sitting beside me 'What do you think of all this?'

She said, as I thought she would, 'They are perfectly entitled to say what they think but they should set up their own campaign rather than expect to use the Association to promote their views'

Well, I thought, the new committee members will have an opportunity to say what they want and we can take it from there.

Following the meeting, 290 parents were asked to vote about the continuation of the Steering Committee of Solicitors; 123 votes were received, of which 102 were in favour and 19 against. Parents were also asked to vote on the names put forward for membership of the Association's Committee; 112 voted in favour and 12 voted against.

Although it was important for parents to know the names of the Committee members who might be working on their behalf, it was never suggested that the Committee should be anything other than a working party. Since there was no formal Association constitution, with rules of procedure and voting rights, all any appointed Committee could do was related to campaigning for the benefit of the parents, and there was no question of such a Committee having power to vote me out of office or make drastic changes to the running of the campaign in the name of the Association of Parents.

I then had to try to correct the false impressions created at the meeting which I knew would be passed on to all of those involved in the question of compensation for vaccine damage. To begin with there was the Legal Aid Board – as it was then called – who had funded the Loveday case and who was being asked by the Steering

Committee to fund a case based on 'bad batches' which Daniel Brennan had suggested as a way forward.

In early September, I attended a meeting with the Legal Aid Board Area Committee, together with Jack Rabinowicz and Patrick Rafferty, the Chairman and a member of the Steering Committee. The first item on our agenda was a letter which the Legal Aid Board had received shortly before our June meeting in which Mr Barr suggested that the Opinion from Daniel Brennan QC was extremely defensive, that there was tension between him and his instructing solicitors and that there was a 'paucity' of instructions. We were able to tell the Legal Aid Committee that, in fact, Daniel Brennan had referred to thousands of pages of judgments, expert research reports and medical literature sent to him in 1995, followed by over 270 pages of medical papers in 1996 and a book entitled *The Adverse Effects of Pertussis and Rubella Vaccines* which ran to 350 pages. If anything, he had been snowed under with paperwork, all of which he had studied in detail before reaching his opinion.

Having attended the meetings with Daniel Brennan, I was also able to report that at all the discussions his manner had been friendly and interested and there was never anything to suggest that his relationship with the instructing solicitors was other than professional.

Turning to the criticisms expressed about the Steering Committee, which represented the parents holding legal aid certificates at the time, I was able to give the results of the poll taken which clearly indicated that the parents in question supported the Steering Committee and its Chairman.

I pointed out that a new Association Committee was being formed and one thing which had been suggested was that the Steering Committee should write to Richard Barr to ask him to discuss his concerns in view of the suggestion put forward at the Association meeting that he should be included in our Steering Committee.

Regarding future legal action, it was planned that the Steering Committee would appoint more medical experts and then go back to Daniel Brennan for a further conference.

It was at this time that it became obvious that the decision to try to take over the campaign and run it with a new Committee, under a different solicitor, had been taken before the June meeting, and that it was now too late to retrieve the situation. When the Board pointed out that any new approach for funding would need to be supported by at least 12 claims, one parent in particular spent some time telephoning around to those who had legal aid certificates inviting them to make up the required number so that the Legal Aid Board would consider his request to be funded.

Then, the new Vaccine Victims Support Group wrote to Association parents, setting out their view on the way forward and inviting parents to contact them for help and advice.

Referring to the meeting, they said, 'Many strong

voices expressed anger and dismay at the direction of the Steering Committee, the lack of action, the poor communication and the years of failure... Our team's legal effort so far has been a disaster.' The letter referred to a 'new generation' of parents and said, 'Together we will win.'

A few parents did join the new Association and most of these were parents who had stopped campaigning after the £10,000 payment but I was very touched by the messages of support I received from most of the others.

In fact, today, nine years later, the Vaccine Victims Support Group has not yet succeeded in obtaining large payouts. The Government is adamant that it will not pay further compensation. The vaccine manufacturers insist that any payment is a matter for the Government. The Legal Services Commission refuse to give aid for any legal action and scientists have not produced any research results which can scientifically prove vaccine damage to the satisfaction of the Court.

As a result of this, a number of the cases on Jack's list disappeared, but he continued to represent the remainder, together with one 'bad batch' case which he pursued for a number of years.

Richard Barr's office at the time was at Dawbarns, King's Lynn. Shortly afterwards, he moved to Hodge Jones and Allen in London, and took with him the cases he had on MMR vaccination, as well as the DPT cases. In June 1998, he wrote to his clients and contacts to brief them on this new arrangement. By 1999, he had again moved to the firm of Alexander Harris Solicitors in Altrincham, Cheshire, where he continued to deal with the investigations into possible legal action in the whooping cough cases until finally withdrawing from the work in 2004.

We had never been told what better information the new solicitors had on which to base a new investigation of the DPT cases, and all of us concerned about the issue were left patiently waiting for further details. The MMR cases were a separate issue, which were being dealt with exclusively and, after being initially involved in the collection of some reports from parents who said their children were damaged by the MMR vaccination, I was not involved in the parents' campaign, which was being very efficiently run by Jackie Fletcher of the JABS group.

I was asked by Richard Barr in September 1996 if I would support the legal action in the MMR cases, but I had to say that my only involvement would be to send details of any cases which appeared to indicate a serious reaction on to the Medicines Control Agency for study. I said at the time, and continued to say, that whereas there were cases of reaction to MMR – particularly those which suggested that the measles vaccine was responsible – which could be said to be 'provable' by expert guidelines, I could not see how an expert report which said, and continued to say, that 'the vaccination did cause autism and bowel disease but that the expert could not prove it' would be pursued by the Government.

Early in 1998, the legal aid certificates on all of

Richard Barr's cases were withdrawn, apparently because the Legal Aid Board wanted clearer details of the basis of the claims. Our Steering Committee was asked to hand over all the reports and papers on which it had based the approach to Counsel to the solicitors now seeking to take over the legal action from them.

It wasn't until November 1998 that the Legal Aid Board reinstated legal aid to the DPT cases Richard Barr had on his file and it was to be another year before the practice he had then joined, Alexander Harris Solicitors, received authority to obtain a Leading Counsel's further opinion as to whether the litigation could be reopened, with the proviso that the two firms of solicitors, Teacher Stern & Selby and Alexander Harris, should be involved in further approaches to Counsel.

In a January 2000 letter from the Legal Aid Board, they stated that it was their intention and the intention of the Area Committee that instructions should be given to Counsel who held the confidence of most (if not all) of the parents concerned and also of the instructing solicitors. It was also the intention, the letter added, that any draft instructions were to be prepared by both Jack Rabinowicz and Alexander Harris, who were then to send the drafts to each other for comment and any amendment.

Altogether it was to take five wasted years after the June 1997 meeting, during which there were meetings with three more QCs, before a final decision on legal action was taken by the Legal Aid Board, which changed nothing from the 1997 position.

I know from discussions I had with Richard Barr at the time that he was genuinely concerned about the damage suffered by the children and that he wanted to fight for their rights. I thought it was a great pity that he did not join in with the Association's Steering Committee solicitors.

The attempt to split the parent campaign group started within days of the June meeting when the rival organisation wrote to Association members telling them that 'many strong voices at the meeting had expressed anger and dismay at the direction of the steering committee, the lack of action, the poor communication and the years of failure. Our team's legal action so far has been a disaster,' the letter added and finished by saying they were willing to listen and help any parent who would like to talk to them at any time.

Days after the letter, I had numerous telephone calls from parents. I wrote back immediately to mention the criticisms at the meeting and to reassure everyone that our campaign would go on as normal.

This wasn't to be the last time that parents were upset by letters and telephone calls about the Association campaign, and were even subject to personal visits seeking their support for a new leader. Since the membership list was registered under the Data Protection Act, I eventually found it necessary to threaten that if the use of the list to contact parents did not stop, I would refer the matter to the Data Protection Registrar.

This unpleasant interference was very upsetting. It was difficult to have to explain it to the parents and the last thing I wanted was to involve them in any personal bickering. I kept my own feelings about the attempts to undermine me in this way to myself, I have always been very concerned that parents should not be misled about either the progress of the campaign, or the likely outcome of our parliamentary or legal efforts. I did not believe that another approach by another group could achieve large-scale provision for vaccine-damaged children, as well as compensation payments for the families, which was what the new group was proposing.

When I got home from the meeting that day I was very tired and fed up. David poured me a drink and said, 'Don't be silly. Carry on with your own plans. Think of the widespread influential support you have among the Ministers you have met and the MPs who continue to support the campaign. Above all, think of Jack Ashley who is still working on your behalf.'

Jack Rabinowicz was also helpful and encouraging. He probably had as much reason as I had to be upset but he maintained a professional attitude at all times and I tried to do the same.

Trying to keep the peace and avoid unpleasantness, I arranged a meeting of the newly elected committee as quickly as possible. We met at the Victory Services Club in August for a preliminary discussion about organisation, roles and procedures. It was a pleasant meeting, I thought, and I recorded in my diary the following day that it was an intelligent committee which could prove very helpful. Afterwards, in an attempt to make sure that everyone was happy and understood the position, I asked the most critical parents to meet me at a local pub for lunch and a drink, where I hoped the atmosphere would be such that we could talk reasonably. I told them that I was still hearing rumours of discontent, that things could not go on like that and they had to accept that I had no intention of retiring from the Association campaign after 20 years. I suggested, in as friendly a way as possible, that if they could not agree with me it would be much better for them to form their own campaign group, publish their aims and plans and see if parents wanted to join them. I even went so far as to say that if they let me have copy of their plans, I would be prepared to circulate them to Association parents.

As a lot of valuable campaign time had been wasted since the May election which had returned a Labour Government, I wanted to press ahead quickly and called the next committee meeting for early November. This would be a full committee of all the Association former members and those recently elected, and I was looking forward to making plans for what I could see would be end of our long-running campaign.

But it was not to be. No sooner had the notice of the meeting gone out, than the arguments and criticisms started all over again. The new committee members didn't like the date I had set and insisted that there should be a detailed discussion with everyone before a date and venue were decided. For me, that was the end. Given the importance of what we were trying to achieve, the suggestion that we should waste time quibbling about who decided the arrangements finished any desire I had to try to liaise with the new members. I confirmed the meeting date to our Association committee and we met as arranged in early November at a local hall.

Ironically, given their first argument about the meeting, the newly proposed committee members and a number of parents they had invited to join them also arranged a meeting for the same day in the same hall, and initially joined us. They did not say why they were there or make any suggestions to resolve any differences. They had brought with them a copy of the informal Association Rules which had been drafted when our Association was formed and which they had previously requested, and they pointed out that this was not a proper constitution. I was very happy to agree that it was not and that it would not help them in any way to vote in a new committee and committee secretary.

Shortly afterwards, they formed the Vaccine Victims Support Group with their own committee. I was then able to get back to the business of the Association campaign, which I was looking forward to seeing through to the end, successfully, and without further trouble.

Cymru, had written to say he would help in any way he could and, after the Easter Recess, I suggested to him that an All-Party Early Day Motion would be the best way of getting support from all sides of the House, to which he agreed.

Dafydd Wigley agreed that an All-Party Motion would be a good idea, and I spent hours on the phone arranging it. I talked to Nick Gibb, Conservative MP for Bognor Regis; to Nick Harvey, Liberal Democrat MP for Devon, North; and to George Stevenson, Labour MP for Stoke-on-Trent, South. Stoke-on-Trent, South had been Jack Ashley's constituency before he became a member of the House of Lords, and it seemed to me that it would be very appropriate if George Stevenson, Jack Ashley's replacement, would act as our principal spokesperson in our newly proposed campaign. The motion, with the four high-profile, all-party signatures was put down in early June 1998 and immediately attracted 83 signatures from all sides of the House of Commons. The Summer Recess at the end of June put an end to the motion, but the signatures were influential in indicating to the Government that our campaign had the support of all sides of the House, and I started to plan a parliamentary campaign to bring the matter to an end.

At the time, Baroness Hollis repeated to all MPs who wrote to her Department about the Vaccine Damage Payment Act that officials had presented Ministers with a range of options which 'would receive due consideration over a period of time which befits a matter of this complexity'. At the same time, the officials had been told that the first priority was to find out about the availability of funds after which a decision would be made about the form of any further payment.

When time passed with no sign of the range of options mentioned, I prepared these myself with the help of my colleagues and included them in an *Options for Improvement* paper in September 1998, which I circulated to MPs, with copies to Ministers. The options open to us were, as I saw it:

1. Implementation of the 1979 recommendation for a system of strict liability. This would have meant that, after the necessary legislation was enacted, parents could go to court without any need to prove negligence and with the possibility of establishing causation 'on the balance of probabilities' similar to the criterion used by the Government in checking claims under the Vaccine Damage Payment Act. This recommendation had been studied and rejected in the House of Lords 20 years previously and I had little hope that it could easily be resurrected.

2. Payment of a sum equal to that which would result from the strict liability system without the need to introduce the necessary legislation. This would require agreement to the payment of anything up to £2 million for each of the 900 claimants and was a sum which I knew that the Government would not consider.

3. Payment of a smaller lump sum to top up existing allowances and to make additional provision similar to the £10,000 payment. Such a sum could be invested to realise an income which, together with amounts included in present benefits for personal allowances, would make a more reasonable contribution to these expenses and make the damaged person less dependent on help from their parents. This was the most popular option and the one which it was felt could be successfully achieved.

4. The setting up of a special fund to which parents could make applications for help; contributors to the fund should be the vaccine manufacturers and the Government. This suggestion had been made to the Government at a meeting in 1996 but they had been unwilling to consider it, saying that any levy on manufacturers would result in higher vaccine prices and that, since the Government purchased all the vaccines, the result would be that the Government would, in effect, be providing the fund.

5. The payment of an exceptionally severe disability pension. This was an idea first proposed in 1979 when the £10,000 payment was made and we suggested that, from age 16 onwards, an additional severe disability pension, similar to war pensions or industrial injuries pensions, should be added to the usual child benefits on behalf of vaccine-damaged children. This would not have provided a lump sum but would have added greatly to the benefits which vaccine-damaged children received.

I had been keeping contact with George Stevenson MP, in the hope that a final parliamentary campaign would be launched after the Summer Recess, backed up by the All-Party Early Day Motion with the *Options for Improvement* paper. I had deliberately kept away from any rumours about splits in the campaign during the summer and I was, therefore, totally unprepared for the news I had from the Department official with whom I had been discussing the *Options for Improvement* paper. Having mentioned that I now needed to get on with organising the parliamentary campaign, she said, 'But haven't you been told that an All-Party MP campaign group has been set up to do this?'

I was speechless. Representatives of the newly formed parent group had gone to visit one of their Manchester supporters – Ian Stewart, MP for Eccles – and at a meeting they arranged at the House of Commons, Ian Stewart had agreed to set up and chair an All-Party Campaign Group; George Stevenson MP, who had also been approached by them, had agreed to join them.

When I wrote to George Stevenson to ask what had happened and why no one had thought to contact me, all he would say was that the whole issue was much too important to be sidetracked by petty arguments, which was true, but it was no answer to the amount of work and effort I had put in to organising an influential Early Day Motion headed by four well-known MPs. I had not indulged in any petty arguments. After all the effort I had put into the work of achieving an All-Party Early Day

Motion of support, I was furious, but short of causing an unseemly squabble which would not have been viewed favourably by MPs, there was nothing I could do. As one MP said, 'The campaign and the children are more important than the personalities.' I agreed with this, but the whole episode destroyed my interest in organising the end of the campaign which, after 25 years' work, was deeply upsetting at the time.

In October 1998, I phoned Ian Stewart MP about the Early Day Motion and he invited me to meet him at the House of Commons. Rene, Sheila and Tony de Groot, a new member of the Committee, went down on the 17th November to discuss our plans and to give him a copy of our Options for Improvement paper.

We were fortunate that Ian Stewart, who went on to lead the rest of the parliamentary campaign, was straightforward and decisive and worked hard to bring the matter to the attention of Parliament at the end of 1998 and again in 1999. Although he was the MP representing some of the parents behind the split in the Association, whether he was aware of this or not, he never allowed it to influence his attitude to any of the campaigning groups and he was courteous and helpful to all. He was aware that the groups had different ideas about what compensation should be paid and he made this clear in his debates to Parliament, saying that any differences did not detract from the overall requirement of Government provision.

By the time the Association had split, and our aims

had diverged, those differences became quite clearly identified. When the Association was formed in 1973, the aim was to get the Government to acknowledge the reality of vaccine damage and to make provision for those who were damaged. This remained the aim right up to the end of the campaign in 2000 and at no time did it vary to take family expenses or special provision for the families themselves into account. Although we had never said what the amount of any payment should be, when £10,000 was paid under the Vaccine Damage Payment Act in 1979, with the statement by David Ennals that this was 'not the end', we knew that any final figure would be a lump sum. We also knew, however, that we were not in a position to sue the Government or anyone else because of the Court's requirement for scientific proof of causation and proof of negligence, and so the amount of any final lump sum would not equal a payment which would be made by the Courts.

The newly formed Vaccine Victims Support Group felt differently, however. Setting up in 1998, in the last two years of the campaign, they were, I believe, influenced by the the observation that very large sums were being paid out for what could sometimes be regarded as minor injuries. To begin with, they felt that vaccine damage should be treated as a medical accident, under which victims and their families were receiving up to £2 million pounds in the late 1990s. It was obvious that Court awards such as these were made on proof of negligence, for which there was punitive compensation as well as provision.

Later, they changed to a demand for 'no fault' compensation, which would pay compensation without proof of negligence. A change in the law would be needed to set up such a scheme, which would, however, still need proof of causation. The group subsequently changed their campaign to what was published as a demand to the vaccine manufacturers to pay £250,000 pounds to each of the 900 families involved, with an ongoing payment of £40,000 each annually.

It was suggestions such as these which kept the groups apart. As with no fault compensation, the law would need to be changed before 'medical accident' compensation could be claimed for vaccine damage and, if schemes like these were introduced, they would obviously date from the day of introduction. The vaccine manufacturers had already been asked by Ministers if they would contribute to a compensation scheme for vaccine damage but the answer was that this would involve an increase in the cost of vaccines and the Government was not prepared to accept such an increase.

I felt, and said, that their suggestions were based more on wishful thinking than on any concrete legal or similar basis and they could not only upset the straightforward campaign based on Government responsibility, but could also lead some of the parents to believe that they might succeed in getting large-scale compensation settlements. In fact, it was the belief by some parents that they would get very large settlements by supporting that campaign that led them to criticise the Association's demands which were thought to be much too limited.

Ian Stewart MP later arranged meetings with all the campaign groups to discuss the way forward. In November 1998 he asked us to meet with the committee of the Vaccine Victims Support Group (VVSG) in a room in the Commons. We had always taken a small committee group to meetings and this time there were only two of us – Sheila and myself. When we got to the room we found that the Support Group had brought five members and had spread out around the conference table so that we had no room to sit down. Ian then had to move us to another room with a bigger table. I had a telephone conversation with one VVSG committee members a few days before the meeting.

'Is it true that you are coming to our meeting with Ian Stewart?' she asked and when I confirmed that it was a joint meeting she went on, 'When you get there I hope you will be careful about what you say. About your option for a pension ...'

I was so cross at that stage that I told her to hang up. 'I have been to more meetings with Ministers than you have,' I said, 'and I do know how to behave.' She wanted to have her say but I ended the conversation quickly and hung up. She was at the meeting but said nothing.

There was a great deal of silence at the meeting and perhaps Ian Stewart was disappointed in what I thought were his sincere efforts to get campaigning groups together to present a united front. It was very clear that there was a great gap between our groups both in what we were trying to achieve and how we were hoping to achieve it.

At the end of the meeting, Ian told us that he had been successful in getting a debate in the House of Commons on 3 December 1998, in which he summarised all the arguments in favour of Government compensation for vaccine damage and urged the Government to take action.

Sitting again in the Strangers' Gallery brought back memories of Jack Ashley's debate nearly 5 years previously. It was interesting to see MPs from all parties taking part and I sat in the gallery wondering what the response from the Minister would be. From past experience, I knew that there would be no statements about procedures and no promises about compensation. In fact, the Minister of State, John Denham, spent three quarters-of-an-hour going back over the history of vaccination promotions and arguing about the MMR claims. I was disappointed to hear him use the Conservative argument that the vaccine-damage payment provided 'substantial preference for children severely disabled as a result of vaccination over children who have been equally severely disabled from some other source'. The whole point of the campaign was that vaccine-damaged children were the direct responsibility of the Government, whereas other severely disabled children, while entitled to Government support, were not. He referred to previous Government statements from the

Department which said that it was hoped to conclude their review of the Payment Scheme early in the New Year. That was as much as we were getting.

In February 1999, all the groups attended a meeting with Hugh Bayley, Parliamentary Under-Secretary of State, Department of Social Security, who was now dealing with the matter. This time the meeting was held in the DSS offices (the old Department of Health and Social Security was now the Department of Social Security, or DSS and later became the Department of Work and Pensions, DWP).

Sheila Casson, Rene Lennon and I attended for the Association and sat in front of a long table beside Ian Stewart, who chaired the meeting and arranged the order of presentations to the Minister, Hugh Bayley, who sat opposite us with his officials. The VVSG committee sat at the far side beside the Minister. I discovered that one of the officials, Geraldine, was Irish but we didn't have much opportunity to talk apart from the standard Irish exchange of details about which part of Ireland one came from. Geraldine stayed as part of the official team dealing with the Association campaign from then on and it was nice to have a friendly face to turn to.

I was reassured to hear Hugh Bayley say that he had studied all the previous presentations carefully and had studied the 1979 report of the Royal Commission which had recommended compensation under a system of strict liability for vaccine damage. I felt he was someone who, with his advisers, would understand the arguments put forward and the principles which prompted them and would do more than give lip service to the presentations.

I repeated the options we had set out, stressing that whatever the final payment was it should not in any way affect the disability benefits and allowances which were being paid. There had been a suggestion after the 1979 payment that the benefits payable then should be reduced and again we said we did not want the Government to 'give with one hand and take away with the other'

The VVSG stressed the need for an urgent answer, repeated the need for no means testing of any payment but didn't at that stage go into any detail about the large lump sum compensation settlements they wanted.

I didn't, of course, expect to hear any definite promise, but at least I left the meeting feeling that progress was being made.

It is an extremely difficult and awkward position to be in when you are putting forward an argument based on years of experience and conviction while sharing the floor with others who have different ideas, different objectives and less overall experience. I had to be very careful to make my own statement and say nothing which showed approval or disapproval of the other statements being made.

There was a tea bar in the offices where we all went after the meeting for tea and sandwiches. Again, we found ourselves sitting at separate tables in the dining room with Ian Stewart moving from one group to another. I must admit that this was probably my fault but any relationship we could have had was spoiled years before when they had tried to undermine me. Anyway, our objectives were now very different and I did not think that they had much hope of achieving theirs.

After the meeting, all the groups were asked to forward any further arguments or submissions which were felt to be relevant but, as far as the Association of Parents was concerned, I felt that all the arguments had been well made over the years. Apart from a short report on the need to ensure that it did not become necessary to pressure the Government into action by detailing their responsibility for the side-effects of polio vaccination, I did not see any need to add to all the existing arguments in favour of our case. As far as a solution to the compensation problem was concerned, I referred to the *Options* paper which I had prepared earlier with the help of committee members, which listed what was possible.

I was at all times in touch with Jack Ashley and although there were no debates in the Lords about the five options, Jack discussed the matter with Ministers. Option three – the payment of a smaller lump sum to top up existing allowances – was the one which I knew could be more quickly achievable and, although we never suggested what the sum should be, we felt it should be at least ten times the original payment.

Hugh Bayley agreed to contact the vaccine manufacturers again about Option Four, but after some delay he informed us that they were not prepared to help. Their argument was, and is, that the Government promotes vaccination and provides the vaccines and that any compensation is a matter for the Government.

Inevitably, as soon as discussions with Ministers about the campaign began, parents who, until that time, had been patiently waiting for progress, became impatient for action and, as 1998 ended and we approached the New Year, we were all desperately hoping for news of the Government's proposals.

Although I was now quite confident that the Government was seriously studying the whole matter, I was well aware that it would take some time yet before the final statement could be made. Ministers were careful to keep pointing out to all queries received that this was an important issue which could not be decided on in haste. They were involving representatives from a wide range of organisations of and for disabled people in considering the scheme and said that consultations between Government departments were also necessary, bearing in mind the complicated and sensitive issues involved, which all takes time.

Although those of us who do not know what goes on in Government from day to day might think it was surely a simple question of deciding on the amount and making a statement, this would obviously be an over-simplification. The cumbersome process of securing Cabinet approval, getting the money from the Treasury, sorting out the legal details and working out the details of the payments themselves wasn't something which could be decided in a matter of weeks or even months.

HELEN'S STORY

In fact, it was to be another 18 months of anxious waiting before we were to hear the Government's response to our campaign for compensation.

18

Deer Hunt

Media interest in the campaign for vaccine-damaged children had waned by this time. *The Times* had been publishing some reports and had been anxious to cover our 1997 meeting, but had been put off by hearing rumours of arguments among the campaigners. Like everyone else, the reporter was reluctant to become involved in petty personal arguments and it was a pity that we lost this influential source of support at the time.

The story of the children themselves had been told many many times and, apart from debates in the House of Commons, there was little new for the media to report. I was therefore intrigued by a telephone call from Brian Deer in August 1998, asking if he could come to see me about an article he was preparing on vaccine damage which he was writing for the *Sunday Times*. He was particularly interested in damage from whooping cough vaccine and wanted to see what details I had. He decided to come up from London by train and I drove to our nearest station, Moreton-in-Marsh, to collect him and bring him back to my home in Shipston-on-Stour.

For an hour or so, he asked questions about the campaign, about how I had collected the cases, about the present position regarding the payment of any compensation from the Government, and about the parent members of the Association of Parents. At some stage, he produced a tape recorder and he also made some notes.

Early on, he referred to the Loveday case, which had been heard in the High Court in 1988, and asked if Susan Loveday's case was one I had dealt with as a possible claim to the Vaccine Damage Payment Unit: I had collected details of over 1,200 such cases prior to 1979, some of which I had filed as 'possible' depending on the clarity of the details given, and others which I had put in a secondary file, which needed more concise details than those given by the parents concerned.

Checking my file, I found that Susan's name was not initially on my list and he seemed to find that interesting. He mentioned the case of Kenneth Best in Ireland and said he had been to see Kenneth's mother, Margaret, and had got a lot of information from her. He also mentioned that he had tried to interview Dr John Wilson, who had refused to take part in an interview with him.

My husband prepared us lunch and the interview continued for nearly four hours altogether, when I drove him back to the station. I wasn't quite sure what kind of article he was considering, and at that stage he didn't say. Unlike most reporters I had met, Brian Deer was not very friendly or chatty. All he wanted was answer to his questions and we had no small talk.

Others coming to the house chatted with David, looked at the photographs, talked about my garden or asked about Shipston. But he kept his head down and just interviewed. I don't even remember him thanking me for taking him to and from the station.

I co-operated as fully as I could because I felt that an article in the *Sunday Times* which would retell the story of vaccine-damaged children would be helpful, particularly at a time when we had the attention of the Government and a promise that they would do something early in the new year.

In Ireland at the time, the Government had decided to launch an investigation into Burroughs Wellcome whooping cough vaccine with particular reference to batch numbers of the vaccine similar to that from which Kenneth Best's vaccination had originated. Members of the Irish Parliament representing their constituents were pressing for such an investigation and Margaret Best was being asked to help. Irish newspapers were contacting her and me for any information which would help them and it was rumoured that there could be other cases similar to Kenneth's taking legal action against the vaccine manufacturer.

I received another phone call from Brian Deer on 9

September 1998, which was sufficiently significant to note in my diary. After a few pleasantries, he said, 'Margaret Best's involvement in the Dublin Government recheck of Burroughs Wellcome vaccines is fraught with danger.'

'What do you mean?' I asked.

'Well, the story could well rebound on Margaret…' He suggested that the Best case might not be as strong as we originally thought. He said, 'Naturally, Burroughs Wellcome was not very happy with the verdict; after all, they had to pay £2.75 million in damages.'

'I'm sorry, but I think that's ridiculous,' I replied. 'Burroughs Wellcome had lawyers and experts in Court, and they weren't a poor firm so they could easily afford the best advisers, so it would be highly surprising if they sat there and allowed a case to proceed which they thought to have been flawed.'

'I understand your point of view,' he said, 'but Burroughs Wellcome were conscious of the fact that everyone in Court and elsewhere regarded Margaret Best as a wonderful parent who had worked hard for a long time to bring her case for her son, and the company felt they would be highly criticised if they contradicted the verdict.'

I found that a bit difficult to believe. Would a highly profitable drug manufacturer like Burroughs Wellcome have allowed a flawed verdict to be brought, and preferred to pay damages of £2.75 million, in addition to the cost of a high-powered team of experts, to avoid public approbation at contesting the verdict? It just didn't make sense.

I telephoned Margaret who confirmed that Brian Deer had been to see her on a few occasions, that she had given him every assistance she could and didn't know what he was talking about.

A month later, on 6 October 1998, my diary entry reads, 'Brian Deer on the phone for 1 hour. Mgt Best later,' meaning that I then telephoned Margaret again.

Then he telephoned and again called into question the strength of the Best case. I argued with him when he made some general comments about the campaign and about some of those involved, and it became a heated discussion.

I couldn't believe what I was hearing. After our interview – which I thought was for an intelligent report of the campaign for vaccine damage – I was arguing with this man about views he was expressing on past events.

By this time I was beginning to worry about Brian Deer and the article he intended to write, and since Margaret Best continued to phone me and was obviously very upset at the possibility that the story was going to try to undermine her case, I agreed that I would telephone Rosemary Conley, the Editor of the *Sunday Times Magazine* in which the article was to appear. I told her in very great detail what Brian Deer had said and suggested that it would not only distress Margaret Best but would also be hotly disputed. Following this, Brian Deer phoned Margaret to assure her that there would be no mention of vaccine batches in the article.

At the time, I was getting ready to go abroad for three weeks and, apart from arranging for someone to buy the paper if it published the article while I was away, there was nothing else I could do. I did, however, include a reference to the article in a Circular of 12 October in which I told parents that it was not, as I thought, an article which would help us but would rather suggest there was no such thing as vaccine damage. I asked parents to watch out for the story and write to the Editor of the *Sunday Times* or to Brian Deer himself to give their views.

Those who read the story did as I asked. One or two decided to phone me instead to complain.

The story appeared in the *Sunday Times Magazine* in early November 1998 and was waiting for me when I got back from my trip. From beginning to end, it was an attack on the campaign that said whooping cough vaccine had caused brain damage in some children. It seemed to ridicule everyone who had been involved in any way with questioning the vaccine thinking. The standfirst on his story relating to Margaret's son Kenneth read as follows:

'THIS MAN WAS BRAIN DAMAGED AS A CHILD. A DRUG COMPANY PAID OUT MORE THAN £2.75M WHEN ITS WHOOPING COUGH VACCINE WAS BLAMED. BUT WHAT IF THE LAW GOT IT WRONG?'

Although the named individuals could obviously be upset, anyone who was used to reading intelligent reports on controversial topics would have to laugh at some of the comments. Dr John Wilson was a respected medical consultant at Great Ormond Street Hospital for Sick

Children, who had published his research into cases of reaction to the vaccine in 1972. Referring to the speech he had given to his medical colleagues at the time, Brian Deer said Dr Wilson had 'polished a fastidious demeanour...', '... he wore a dark suit and gold cufflinks...' and '... read slowly in the voice of a bishop.'

One assumes from such comments that he had been present at the speech 26 years previously, although he did not say so. Dr Wilson had refused his request for an interview.

His next reference was to Margaret Best who had just won the £2.75 million settlement from Burroughs Wellcome and whom he had recently visited. Margaret was, he said, 'living like a lottery winner in a five-bedroom house... ' which had 'electric gates, a gravel drive, floodlights and barking dogs'. The fact that she had fought hard for the money in order to provide lifetime care in her home for her disabled son, and that security measures around the house were needed to protect someone with no awareness of danger, was not mentioned. The reference to a 'lottery winner' was particularly unpleasant.

He then moved on to Professor Gordon Stewart, one of a panel of six experts set up by the Government to look at the questionnaires I had prepared about events following whooping cough vaccination in 229 children. One of these cases, the Kinnear case, went to Court but could not proceed because there was contradictory evidence from the parents about the events after vaccination. Professor Stewart, who was dealing with the case, became caught up in the arguments and unfairly bore the brunt of the subsequent criticism. Deer referred to him as 'this white haired professor'.

When he referred to the next Court case, the Loveday case, he went into some detail about the Judge's examination of the expert witnesses and the case material and then quoted the Judge's finding as: 'I have come to the clear conclusion that the plaintiff fails to satisfy me on the balance of probability that pertussis vaccine can cause permanent brain damage.' He left out the qualification by the judge, 'It is possible that it does, the contrary cannot be proved.' When I asked him why he had not put that in he said it was a 'double negative' which was not important.

He went back to see Margaret Best once again and this time referred to her 'closed-circuit TV screen monitoring her electric gates' and her 'live-in friend' who had taken Kenneth out for a drive. He spent some time reflecting on what it would be like to have a child like Kenneth, to go through all the trauma involved with hospitals, to wonder from which side of the family the disability came, to worry about what would happen later when he was an adult and, beyond that, when she was dead. He came up with his simple conclusion that, in that situation, it would be 'easy to see why the vaccine and drug companies might be welcome scapegoats'. Brian Deer was, it seems, prepared to plumb any depth of sarcasm and innuendo to advance his argument.

I could barely wait to see what he had written about me. I was last on his list and described as 'a big-framed woman of 70, a farmer's daughter from County Tipperary'. The article did not mention that I had left Ireland in my twenties and could no longer be thought of as a rural farm worker. Having more or less blamed me for initiating the campaign on behalf of drug-damaged children, he was quite clearly anxious not to portray me as either intelligent or sophisticated, so 'a big Irish farmer's daughter' fitted this perfectly.

How times and reporters change, I thought. Twenty years previously I had been described as 'dark haired, talks in a soft Irish accent, radiates calmness and determination and needs every ounce of these two qualities she can muster.' This was by David Bradney, a former science and technology reporter for the *Birmingham Post*, writing in the *New Scientist* on 20 May 1976 following up on Celia Hall's origianl article.

Brian Deer went through the details of the campaign and mentioned some press cuttings in a plastic folder which I had given him at the same time as my husband brought us lunch. 'She made a ham salad and produced a plastic bag... ' was how he worded it.

Up to that point, much of what he had written had simply amused us, but he then went on to discuss Helen's case in more detail, and arranged his questioning in such a way that it would be easy to take the answers out of context. I agreed that I had still not been able to 'show a case', which I meant specifically in the context of

201

providing sufficient evidence to satisfy the Court. Before starting the campaign, I had taken legal advice but the 'proof of causation' issue had arisen then and I had not proceeded. He suggested that my belief that the vaccine causes damage was an article of faith, with which I agreed, because an article of faith is a deeply held belief which does not change, but somehow his wording made it sound like a doubt. I agreed that it was impossible to prove it in Court, but he then suggested that technological advances could make it possible to reassess my daughter's case, clearly implying that this would provide a different diagnosis. I said I would not consider that and, when he probed for a reason, I was led into a discussion of what a different diagnosis would do to the vaccine-damage argument, having been the one to start the campaign.

He very cleverly arranged his report of this to make me look uncertain about my daughter's case, which was not what I had meant to convey at all. Because of that, I referred the article to the Press Complaints Commission, but they ruled against my complaint that he had taken what I had said out of context. I wasn't really surprised as I have little faith in self-regulatory bodies.

It took me some time to get over the surprise of having an article like that – which, in my opinion, would have been better suited to a gossipy tabloid – published by the *Sunday Times*, which in the 1970s had printed informative and intelligent reports by Dr Oliver Gillie. Brian Deer had himself referred to the Oliver Gillie reports and mentioned that Oliver had received a Press Award for the reports at the time. When I asked him if he thought he would get a similar award, he was non-commital, but after I had read his article, I wrote to him to say that he would do well to re-read the Oliver Gillie reports to see how to deal with the issue properly.

In the event, the story did not do us any damage. I heard only one reference to it from a Department of Health spokesman who, naturally, would refute any suggestion that vaccination could be dangerous.

Coming as it did shortly before we were to meet the new Minister, Hugh Bayley, and knowing that at least one official in his Department had referred to the Deer article, it was certainly something we could have done without at the time. We need not have worried, though. Hugh Bayley himself referred to the Loveday Ruling and made a point of quoting it in full, including the qualification.

19

Battling for a Win

The New Year of 1999, which we all thought would see the end of the campaign, came and went. I continued to send lobby letters to MPs but there are only so many ways you can state your case and so many answers to the same question you can get. One interesting copy letter from a member was a reply from Alistair Darling, the Secretary of State for Social Security, to William Hague, who had written in support of our All-Party Early Day Motion 1432, something of a contrast to his own handling of our letters to him when he was Minister for Social Security four years previously. Then, he had said that the Government's view was that the Payment Scheme operated in a 'fair and effective manner – a view which I echo'.

The most interesting response was the letter I got from

Alistair Darling, the Secretary of State, saying that our *Options* paper had been passed to him by Tony Benn and that he appreciated the opportunity to include our suggestions in the ongoing review. It was our Option Three, suggesting a top-up payment, which eventually was accepted. Tony Benn had been a constant supporter of our cause over a number of years and we were all very grateful to him for his direct representation to the Secretary of State.

At the time, there were four campaign groups – something of a change from the Association's lonely battle in the 1970s. There was the JABS Group, set up in 1990 to represent families who said their children had been damaged by MMR vaccines, was run by Jackie Fletcher to whom I had handed over some of those specific cases referred to me at the start of our campaign.

Second was the Justice for All Vaccine Damaged Children Group, initially set up to represent families whose claims had failed. They had campaigned to get the 1979 Payment Act changed so that 'proof of causation' could be changed to 'the benefit of the doubt', but this failed because, as the Government pointed out, such a scheme would not be strictly related to vaccine damage; any child considered to be normal at birth but subsequently found to be damaged without any known cause could claim it might have been the vaccination and be given the benefit of the doubt.

The third organisation was the Vaccine Victims Support Group. The breakaway group had been recently formed by those who had been harshly critical of both the steering committee of solicitors and myself at the June meeting. They wanted to launch a new campaign to win large-scale compensation, not only for vaccine-damaged children, but for the families as well.

The last of the four bodies was the Polio Group. I had not heard anything of this group until we met their secretary at the June meeting with Hugh Bayley. Their main concern was young children who had contracted polio from the live virus oral polio vaccine.

Throughout the year there was constant publicity about the MMR vaccination but little, if any, about the Government's plans for compensation. The MMR group was planning legal action but it seemed that there was little chance of the Association doing the same for the whooping cough cases. The Legal Aid Board had funded Alexander Harris Solicitors to obtain another Counsel's opinion.

Then, early in 2000, I had a phone call from a *Daily Express* reporter who said that the paper was anxious to cover the vaccine-damage compensation story and asked for background literature. I sent on the details and facts about the campaign, covering briefly our four-year successful campaign from 1974 to 1978, and our long-running campaign from 1978 onwards, which had failed to get the Conservative Government to add to the original payment, and our promising contacts with the new Labour Government which I was sure would end in success. Although I wasn't entirely convinced that a very public press campaign was necessary, I felt that publicity would be useful to let everyone know what was going on.

The *Daily Express* publicity campaign started in May 2000 and went on for two months. I had fully expected that there would be a lead into their stories by way of a report about the Association's 1970s campaign and the Vaccine Damage Payment Act, which now required amendment to increase the payment and ease some of the restrictions involved. I also expected some mention of the 20-year struggle to get the Act amended and the parliamentary debates which went into this effort from 1979 to 1996.

When all this was ignored and the stories started as if the *Daily Express* had suddenly discovered the flaws in the Payment Act and was now launching a 'New Campaign for Vaccine Damaged Children'.

I decided to call the reporter responsible for the story, saying, 'I'm really surprised at the way in which you are reporting the issue. And I want to make it clear, I'm not in the least interested in personal references, but I do feel that, having asked for background material which I sent you urgently, you might at least have discussed the story with me.'

'I would have thought,' she replied, 'that you would be more interested in pursuing the matter in the interests of the children concerned, rather than quibbling about the content of the story.'

After the exchange, I did not feel that I could continue my co-operation.

From May 2000 until the Government announcement on 20 June, the *Express* ran more or less daily reports covering the plight of many of the families with vaccine-damaged sons and daughters. These were sympathetic and gave details of the miseries suffered by the parents concerned. In some cases, they were sensational. At one stage, I was very worried about the paper's concentration on an Early Day Motion supported in 1986 by Gordon Brown and by the critical comments about Mr Brown included in the article. Here we were, hoping that the Treasury, of which Mr Brown was Chancellor, would agree to release funds to increase the Vaccine Damage Payment in co-operation with his friend, Alistair Darling, Secretary of State for Social Security, and there were people crudely telling him to 'put his money where his mouth is'. It would not have been surprising if Mr Brown had been tempted to refuse to consider the matter at all but, hopefully, I thought, Mr Brown wasn't a reader of the *Daily Express*. As became evident shortly afterwards, at the time these stories were written, he was, in fact, agreeing to release up to £60 million pounds for additional payments for vaccine damage.

I followed most of these stories while I was in Ireland on a holiday/business trip. When I read on the 30 May the reference by the Editor to 'the disgusting Vaccine Damage Payment Scheme' and 'the grubby payment scheme', I was incensed. It is so easy for people coming into campaigns at the last moment to make quick judgements about what has gone before, or what they feel should have happened or how they think they would have handled the problem better.

I telephoned Sheila Casson to ask her to send a letter to the *Daily Express* to make the point that, although the Payment Scheme might be inadequate and restricted, it was unique in acknowledging, for the first time, that vaccines could cause damage and that Governments had responsibility for such damage. Publicity about the scheme had, I said, led to successful campaigns for compensation for vaccine damage in Canada, the United States, New Zealand and Australia and that, without the Payment Scheme, the chances of any compensation campaign succeeding today would be slim. The paper published this under the headline 'VACCINE ACT A TRAILBLAZER FOR COMPENSATION RIGHTS' which made me feel a bit better about what they were doing.

It was left to Hugh Bayley, Minister of State at the Department, to set the record straight. Answering a debate on the subject on 6 June 2000, shortly before the final announcement of the increase in the payment, he made a particular point of referring to the campaign which had resulted in the legislation covering the original lump sum, paying tribute to Jack Ashley, Alfred Morris and me as the campaigners who had achieved this, and adding that, without this campaigning, the Vaccine Damage Payment Act would never have reached the statute book and – by implication – that there would therefore be no amendment to debate. I wasn't present to hear the debate, but I wrote to him afterwards to thank him for his comments.

When newspapers take up a cause and follow it for some months until there is a successful resolution of the problem concerned, they do like to suggest that it was their publicity which achieved the success. Following the announcement by Alistair Darling on 27 June 2000 of the increase in the Vaccine Damage Payment to £100,000, the *Express* announced the next day that 'it took our campaign to force the Government to increase compensation to vaccine-damaged children'. To my mind, they had no right whatsoever to claim the victory. Bearing in mind that their publicity had only started six weeks earlier, it is reasonable to suggest that all the necessary Ministerial decisions, agreements and arrangements for funding were already in place and that, at best, the publicity highlighted the need for a Ministerial statement.

The day after the Government announcement, there was a public lobby of Parliament by the Vaccine Victims Support Group, supported by the *Daily Express*. The payment was welcomed but was said to fall a long way short of justice. A 'no fault' compensation scheme funded by the vaccine manufacturers was now proposed, so that there would be no need to go to Court for further provision.

20

Settling Up

Earlier in our campaign, I had asked Hugh Bayley, Parliamentary Under-Secretary of State at the DHSS, if he would give me some advance warning of any statement to be made by the Secretary of State about compensation. He said he would consider it, but I wasn't confident that he would as I knew only too well that statements to the House on issues like this are never leaked beforehand, and that any mention of the date might start questions and rumours.

It was Jack Ashley who telephoned me on Tuesday morning, 27 June 2000, to say that the statement for which we had both waited for so long was to be made by Alistair Darling, Secretary of State for Social Services, that afternoon. I wanted to go down to the House of Commons to listen to it, but as so often happened on important occasions, I was unable to do so and spent some time wondering how to arrange to hear Alistair Darling as he spoke. My youngest daughter who lived in Wimbledon had a television on which she was able to receive live broadcasts from Westminster, so I established a link by telephoning her and asking her to put the phone close to the television, and that was how I heard the statement which was to be the glorious end to a 26-year campaign for vaccine-damaged children.

Alistair Darling began by describing the 1979 Vaccine Damage Payment Act and two of its rules – the time limit of six years in which claims had to be made, and the required 80 per cent degree of disability. Regarding the time limit, he said that this was too short in respect of young children who account for the vast majority of claims, and referring to the degree of disability, he said he would reduce this to 60 per cent.

Regarding the lump sum payable under the Act, he said this would be raised to £100,000 for all new cases, a surprisingly generous increase, I thought, while holding my breath to see what he would propose for the 900 established cases which had formed the basis of all the campaigning and pressure which had achieved the 1979 Act, and had led up to the amendments now being discussed.

'I can announce,' Alistair Darling went on, 'that those who have already received lump sums will get top-up payments so that they are put on an equal footing in real terms with new claimants.' For most of the 900 past claimants who got £10,000 under the Payment Act – the present-day value of which the Government assessed as £32,000 – this meant a top-up of £68,000 each, bringing the total to £100,000.

I cannot describe the immense relief I felt on hearing this statement. We now had an answer to all our prayers and an end, I thought, to our 26-year campaign. Although Alistair Darling had mentioned 'young children' in his reference to the changes to the six-year limit and the disability requirement, he had responded to a question about those who would now be over the age of 21 by saying, 'I want to ensure that people are not unfairly excluded simply because they do not come within the new scheme ... I want to avoid the situation in which someone who would qualify now is barred because of the old rules.' This took care of everything, I thought; those whose claims were turned down in the past because their claims were late, or because they were not 80 per cent disabled, could now reapply.

When compared to what could be awarded following a successful Court action, £68,000 was a small sum, although I felt that it was a reasonable settlement in the circumstances. Counsel's opinion was that proof of causation would be a prime requirement for any approach to the Court and, at that time, and even to date, there were no scientific studies on which it would be possible to show the Court precisely how damage occurred following the administration of the vaccines in question. Proof on the balance of probabilities was all that was required for claims made under the Payment Act, but this was not sufficient for the Court.

The payment was also a top-up to enable families to provide better care for their damaged sons and daughters, many of whom were settled in residential accommodation while others lived at home. For those who lived in residential homes, all of whose living costs were met by the State, there had always been an urgent need for funds to provide for extras such as holidays; recreational outings and facilities; transport to enable home visits to be made or to help families to visit; decent clothes and personal items and any other comforts needed to enhance the quality of life. Until the top-up payment was received, most of these costs had been paid by the families, as the only other amount available to the vaccine-damaged person was the princely sum of about £16 a week, which was supposed to cover all the extra expenses. Today, this personal allowance has risen to a staggeringly pitiful £18.10 per week.

There were some families who longed to be able to make their own long-term arrangements for the care of their disabled child at home, to build special accommodation and arrange for reliable staff, so that parents would not have to worry about what happened when they died. Clearly, the amount required to do this would be vastly greater than the amount of the top-up payment and the families concerned were highly critical of it. However, short of a breakthrough in the problem about scientific proof of causation, which would enable these parents to go to Court and successfully claim a Court award, it is difficult to see how their problem will be resolved.

The day following the statement in the Commons, hundreds of parents phoned in to say how pleased they were at the news. Flowers kept arriving all day followed by some beautiful gifts, amongst which was a china Lladro dancing girl and a Caithness red glass 'wise owl' with its card which read 'I don't give a hoot'. These and many other gifts continue to remind me of my close contact with the parents who joined me in the campaign.

That day I sent an e-mail to Ministers at the Department to pass on these sentiments. That evening, on 28 June 2000, I went with my husband to the House of Lords to meet Jack and Pauline Ashley and to listen to the debate on the Vaccine Damage Payment which Jack introduced. He was joined by a number of Lords, including Lord Brennan, most expressing satisfaction but one or two critical of the amount and one or two Conservative Peers critical of what they said was the delay in introducing the beneficial amendment to the Payment Act. Considering the number of years we had criticised the Conservative refusal to do anything, I found that somewhat ironic.

The debate was answered by Baroness Hollis, who had previously been closely involved in the discussions about the issues raised and who also referred to cases which might fall outside the 21-year cut-off point, saying the Government aimed to make the new provisions fair to people who had missed out in the past and who may qualify under the new rules.

At the end of the debate, Baroness Hollis included in her speech the email I had sent on behalf of the Association, referring to it as a graceful and gracious message. On that note, an exciting evening, which had brought a successful conclusion to our efforts of the previous 26 years, ended.

From then until December 2000, I was kept busy telling parents about the payments, checking their names and changes of address, and answering various queries which arose about the payments from time to time. One of the points we had made in discussions with the Department was that any payment made should not affect the benefits being paid to the disabled person. It should not, we said, give with one hand and take away with the other, an argument we had previously made in 1979, when the benefit rules were such that there was a danger that keeping the money invested for the future use of the disabled child would mean a cut in the disability benefits available.

To answer the queries being raised about the possible effect of the payment on available disability benefits, the Benefits Agency issued helpful leaflets which I could pass on. These gave comprehensive details and, in the majority of cases, where local benefit offices were concerned about the use of the payment, parents were able to show that the money was intended for purposes other than the provision of services covered by the benefits. It was clear from the Deed of Trust which accompanied each payment that this was a Discretionary Trust, which was one where the beneficiary has no right to payments nor any right to say how the trust should be administered. Payments are made at the discretion of the Trustees. The beneficiaries were, of course, mostly disabled and unable to manage their own affairs. There were a few cases, though, where DSS benefit officers did not at first appreciate the difference between these payments and others where beneficiaries had absolute entitlement to the money in Trust, and a few parents were very upset by being told that they had to 'account for every penny they spent' or 'provide complete details, with receipts, when they bought anything'. With the help of the leaflets which the Payment Unit provided, and with the help in some cases of the Payment Unit Staff, we did manage to resolve these queries eventually.

By the spring of 2001, things were settling down again. Many parents had received the payment and made suitable arrangements for banking it. Many took the first decent holiday they would have been able to have with their disabled child for years and were able to buy some help. Some were able to make some badly needed alterations to their accommodation. I particularly remember the joy of a parent who lived in a small house with an upstairs bathroom, who was able to build a downstairs toilet to save having to help her disabled son upstairs numerous times a day. This was really what the campaign for provision had been all about and it made all the work and effort by all involved worthwhile.

So was it all worthwhile?

If Helen's story is anything to go by, the payment has made a big impact on the lives of those who were vaccine damaged. Most of those for whom the Association was originally formed are now adults, some still living at home and some, like Helen, in residential accommodation.

When it started, all they had was a very small pocket money allowance and parents had to dig into their own resources to top this up. Today, Helen has her vaccine damage payment invested in such a way that most of it is safe to pay for any large costs which may arise in the future, when she may need medical or other care. Part of it, however, is invested to provide an ongoing income.

She can now afford nice holidays. She travels by air to France to have holidays with her youngest sister, Rosanna and her niece Holly and nephew Joel. We drive her to Wimbledon to see her eldest sister, Suzanne and her nephews, Liam and Daniel. She loves to sit and watch them playing.

She is able to buy nice clothes, sometimes with my help but more often with the help of her care worker, Carol, who is a better judge of what is modern and suitable for Helen's age group. She can buy extra things in her home such as her own special chair, a radio and TV and her own furniture for her bedroom.

She has short breaks at a nearby Country Club where she enjoys saunas and massages, with first class accommodation.

While her doctors and specialists are always available to

see her and the local hospital has provided care for her, she could afford urgent private medical consultations if these became necessary.

Were funding of her care home ever to change, necessitating moving to another care facility, the money would help her to make or improve the arrangements.

In the long term, while Helen's sisters will look after her interests and visit to check on her welfare, they do not live nearby. The money will ensure that a local Advocate can be appointed to keep in touch with them.

So yes, for Helen the campaign was worthwhile and I know that many others say the same.

21

A Voice for the Forgotten Few

Inevitably, the publicity about the amendment to the Act and about the increased payment brought queries from those whose claims had been turned down under the 1979 Act because they had not claimed within the six years specified, or because the claim was for someone considered to be less than 80 per cent disabled. I had held a small file of such cases over the years and now started to see what action was needed to pursue them in the light of the new legislation.

Legislation had not been necessary for the distribution of the top-up payments but it was required for changes to the 1979 Act regarding the six-year limit for receipt of claims and changes to the disability percentage. In the past, such legislation would have required debates in the House of Commons and in the Lords, followed by the introduction of a Bill covering these amendments, all of which would have been published and would have given everyone an opportunity to comment. However, in this instance the Government decided to introduce the changes to the Vaccine Damage Payments Act by way of a Regulatory Reform Order as provided for by the recent Regulatory Reform Act 2001. The Reform Order requires a consultation on the proposed legislation followed by an extended scrutiny by Committees in the House of Parliament.

The rule about the Consultation is that it has to be a thorough and effective consultation with interested parties. The Minister is expected to seek out actively the views of those concerned, including those who may be adversely affected and demonstrate to the scrutiny committees that these concerns have been addressed.

The Consultation Document covering changes to the 1979 Act was issued by the Department for Work and Pensions in July 2001. This invited comments on the proposals later laid before Parliament in June 2002. The first of these was to change the six-year limit for making claims, which Alistair Darling had said was too short in respect of young children, and enable claims to be made up to age 21. Second, it outlined changes to the disability threshold from 80 to 60 per cent. And it included a new proposal which had never been before been presented to Parliament, to allow claims which fell outside Proposals One and Two – i.e. previous claims under the 1979 Act – provided the claims 'satisfied the proposed new rule'.

Nowhere did it say clearly what the proposed new rule for old claims was, and what we were relying on was the statement made by Alistair Darling in Parliament which said, 'I want to ensure that people are not unfairly excluded simply because they do not come within the new scheme. I want to avoid the situation in which someone who would qualify now is barred because of the old rules...'

Responding to the Consultation Document on behalf of the Association, I first missed the implications of Proposal Three because of the way it was worded, and commented that the amendments proposed were beneficial. When I was later advised that the proposed new rule meant that older claims could only be considered if the claimant was under 21 at the time of the claim, I immediately changed my submission and wrote to the Department of Work and Pensions to say that the requirement about satisfying the proposed new rule in older claims should be removed. In all the years of the Association's campaign, our prime concern had been amendments to the Payment Act which would benefit all those who had campaigned for the payment rather than amendments for the benefit of future generations. Since the Payment Act covered vaccine damage from 1948 onwards, it was obvious that, in 2000, some of the older claims barred under the old rules would again be barred by the new ones.

The Consultation Document went out to 59 consultees. There were only 13 responses, 11 of whom fully replied to most but not all of the questions posed, while 2 had no view about any of the points involved – a response rate of only 18 per cent.

A Statement by the Department for Work and Pensions laid before Parliament on 14 January 2002 included details of the amendments announced in Parliament by Alistair Darling in June 2000 and of the Consultation responses to be considered by the Regulatory Committees.

Although I had not received any response from the Department about my submission that Proposal Three should be amended, I saw that it was included in the report of the consultation responses, but tucked away in the middle of three pages of Department comment.

Never mind, I thought, the Scrutiny Committees will read all the submissions and be aware of all the arguments but, just to make sure that they would be aware of what I saw as errors and inconsistencies in the Department's Statement, I wrote to the Clerk to the Committee in March to set these out.

I heard nothing about the deliberations of the Deregulation and Regulatory Reform Committee between January and March 2002, when their report entitled *Proposal for the Regulatory Reform (Vaccine Damage Payments Act 1979) Order 2002* was published. The Press Notice which was issued on 20 March 2002 referred to a suggestion that an amendment was necessary before the Order was laid before the House of Commons, so I rushed to get a copy of the Committee's report to see what was proposed, hoping that it might relate to the amendments we wanted.

The Report just repeated the Department's reference to what they said had been announced in Parliament. The reference to the 'proposed new rule' was repeated but not explained. The Consultation was said to be 'adequate with a broad level of support for the proposals'.

The report referred to the detailed arguments which I had made to the Committee about the manner in which the proposed new rule had been introduced into the Consultation Document and my suggestion that the age 21 rule for past claimants should be removed from the proposals. The Committee said they had not considered it appropriate to examine the merits of these points since their concern was matters of policy unconnected with regulatory reform criteria. The Committee were 'satisfied that the proposals take adequate account of the responses to consultation.'

It was impossible either to understand or accept this. A Government Department had produced three Proposals for amending an Act of Parliament, one of which had not been discussed in Parliament, had not been properly described or explained in the Consultation Document or publicly discussed with anyone else. And here was the Committee set up to examine the Proposals and the Consultation Document to decide if the Government should proceed, saying that it could not consider any public arguments against the proposals because they were matters of policy.

At that stage, I could not see what purpose if any the Regulatory Reform Committee served, and neither could

I see the validity of a consultation exercise which collected comments and arguments which were not subjected to any independent scrutiny but were answered by the Department involved in the amendment process. I became even more convinced of that view when I discovered that even before the Consultation Document was issued in 2001, letters were sent to parents whose unsuccessful claims under the 1979 Act were held by the Department and who were enquiring about the new legislation. They were told that to be considered under the revised legislation their claims would have had to be made before the claimants twenty-first birthday. These letters went out twelve months before there was any announcement in Parliament about the new legislation and none of these parents were told about the Consultation process. A total of 251 claimants were dismissed in this way and, as far as I was concerned, the whole consultation process was a farce.

Later, the Regulatory Reform Committee issued a report in which they referred to their inability to consider representations made on behalf of the Association parents who would be barred by the under-21 rule. They said that a Member of Parliament could question the Government about any aspect of its proposals, and I then asked Ian Stewart MP to raise the issue with the Committee and arrange a meeting with Maria Eagle, the Secretary of State, to question the way in which our representations had been dealt with. Ian Stewart thought this could be an embarrassment for the

Minister and that the matter might be better dealt with by a meeting in her office.

I saw the meeting as an opportunity to express concern and dissatisfaction at the way in which the whole matter had been dealt with, and to see what might be done to amend the legislation regarding the time limit for past cases.

It was a pleasant meeting which achieved nothing, apart from the Minister's promise to look at any claims where it was felt that people had been put at a disadvantage. However, since anyone who felt they had a claim but could not make it under the new rules was at a disadvantage but would still not be able to claim, this was a meaningless offer.

I continued to write to the Minister, as did Jack Ashley and individual MPs representing about 50 families on my file who were adversely affected by the legislation, but to no avail. A Judicial Review of Proposal Three and the way in which the whole consultation process was handled was considered as a way of helping these families, some of whom desperately wanted to be given the opportunity to tell their stories, and many went to great lengths to try to find the medical and other details necessary for a claim. Obviously, this was very difficult, given that the vaccinations had occurred anything up to 30 years previously in some cases, and that very few medical records were still available, but it had to be clear that they might have a good chance of making a successful claim.

The advice I was given was that a Judicial Review would

be possible but that it would require a strong claim which could demonstrate that a refusal to allow it would be unjust. Such a claim, of course, would have to be able to show, on the balance of probabilities, that the vaccination caused the damage but, after carefully checking all the details which the parents had, it was clear that this was not enough to make a successful claim. Given the situation in which there was no scientific proof of causation acceptable to the Courts at the time, this was a further difficulty for anyone talking about proving vaccine damage.

A Judicial Review of the way in which the Department had introduced an age 21 rule for past cases might succeed in overturning the rule, but there would be little point in that if the claims then failed to prove causation,

At that stage, I was then reluctantly forced to write to the parents on the file which I had held for so long to say that there was nothing further I could do for them.

In April 2003, I wrote to the Minister to repeat all the arguments I had made about the way in which the Vaccine Damage Payment Scheme had been amended – that it had deprived some parents of any hope of making a claim. Reminding her that the Association of Parents had campaigned for 20 years for a removal of the six-year limit in the 1979 Act so that everyone could at least have a claim examined, I said that the action taken in relation to that particular issue was arbitrary, discriminatory and unjust, but I had to conclude by saying that I would not pursue the matter further.

Before Regulatory Reform arrangements were first introduced, Government Ministers announced their proposals in Parliament. MPs had an opportunity to question them and, representing the particular concerns of their constituents, were able to argue about the proposals which might be detrimental to their welfare. Media interest ensured that those with an interest in the subject were kept informed and given an opportunity to comment. With the introduction of Regulatory Reform – at least in the case of vaccine-damaged children – Departments were able to put forward their own proposals, monitor the consultation reports themselves and, having no independent body to argue against them, make their own decisions and make sure they became law. The Regulatory Reform Committees to whom the consultation reports were sent and who would, I thought, have acted as a judge between the Department's proposals and the views of interested parties, did not become involved in what they saw as matters of policy. So what we were left with were decisions taken by the DWP in the wake of the Statement to Parliament in June 2000 about which no argument would prevail.

I am still of the opinion that the manner in which the 1979 Act was amended should be the subject of review to see if the Department should have been able to make arbitrary decisions which were never announced in Parliament, and whether they should have ignored the Code of Conduct for Consultations.

However, since my purpose was to act for parents who

would not have been helped by the outcome of any such review, I had to decide to reluctantly end my campaign on the subject.

The Association's campaign, which had started in 1973 with the help of Jack Ashley and, subsequently, other MPs who had stepped in to help, had seen an acceptance by the Government that when national immunisation programmes which protected the nation from disease occasionally caused individual damage, special Government provision for the damaged was required. It had seen a 1979 payment of £10,000 increased to £100,000, and seen an improved scheme for those to be vaccinated in the future. It had seen a few families deprived of a chance to claim, but nearly 1,000 families received a reasonably satisfactory sum to help them provide extras for their damaged sons and daughters to enable them to experience a better quality of life. At the end of the enquiry about the Consultation process in April 2003, the Parliamentary campaign for vaccine damaged children came to an end.

22

Cases Dismissed

I t was then time to turn to the solicitors who had been
considering legal action to see what, if any, solution
there might be for the parents who wanted to pursue
this course.

Back in December 1996, Daniel Brennan QC, the
Counsel in the Loveday case, had given as his opinion to
Jack Rabinowicz and the Association Steering Committee
that, before any new case could be brought, it would be
vital to produce fresh evidence bearing on causation, and
his view was that there was no adequate material to take
the question of causation further.

He was, however, of the view that there was a sufficient
basis for further investigation of defective batch claims,
similar to the Best case in Ireland.

It was this opinion which had caused the controversy at
our June 1997 meeting and which had prompted Richard

Barr, with the backing of some parents with legal aid certificates, to seek legal aid for another Counsel's opinion based on what he said was better information available to him.

In the Spring of 1998, legal aid was withdrawn from all the cases which had been transferred to Richard Barr, and it was only in November 1998 that the Legal Aid Board reversed its decision and returned legal aid to the cases in question. For the firm in question, Alexander Harris Solicitors, it was to be another year before they were authorised to instruct Counsel who held the confidence of most if not all the parents concerned. The Board said that Jack Rabinowicz was to be closely involved in the selection and briefing of Counsel, and the two firms of solicitors were to exchange drafts and details of any amendments.

In May 1998, the solicitors consulted Daniel Serota QC and Caroline Harry Thomas of Counsel and the attendance note shows that Daniel Serota advised the solicitors that evidence showing a causal link between vaccination and brain damage was essential.

In July 2000, the solicitors consulted Simeon Maskrey QC and, again, his opinion rested on the question of causation; if the evidence existed that the vaccine could cause damage, all actions could proceed. Otherwise, none of the actions can proceed.

It was clear from the outcome of discussions between solicitors and medical experts that there was no established scientific method of proving causation.

In 2001, the Legal Aid Board, now known as the Legal Services Commission, decided to go back to Daniel Brennan QC to get an independent opinion about the current state of investigation into, and assessment of, the merits of further whooping cough litigation for which Alexander Harris had been given legal aid.

Daniel Brennan now had the new Counsels' opinions to study and he began by comparing the instructions given to Simeon Maskrey QC by Alexander Harris Solicitors and those given to him in 1996 by Jack Rabinowicz . He was satisfied that the details with which he had been supplied were of a high standard and provided him with all the information he required to enable him to give a firm opinion. He went into considerable detail about aspects of the law and various medical and other reports discussing cases of vaccine damage and he answered criticisms made about the quality of the instructions he had been given before he reached his 1996 opinion. His opinion to the Legal Services Commission was given in September 2001.

His conclusion was that any fresh investigation into vaccine damage could only be justified on the basis of convincing new evidence materially bearing on the issue of causation. This was true whether claims were advanced because of negligence or under the Consumer Protection Act. There was no such new evidence, he said, and therefore he concluded that legal aid should not be granted for further investigation of the claims.

Following this, a conference took place with Lord

Brennan in September 2002 at which he was provided with further material for his consideration. The conference was attended by representatives from Alexander Harris Solicitors, Hodge Jones and Allan, Teacher Stern and Selby and Irwin Mitchell. Following his study of all the new material provided, Lord Brennan gave his further opinion to the Legal Services Commission on 9 January 2003, which was that, on the material available, the causation issue should be considered closed and that it was not justified to grant legal aid for any further litigation.

The Legal Services Commission informed solicitors that they were entitled to make representations against any decision to discharge current legal aid certificates, promising that they would consider any such representations. They added that if, despite any representations received, they remained of the opinion that the certificates should not be continued, they would proceed to discharge.

Alexander Harris Solicitors did make representations to oppose the discharge of existing certificates in April 2003 on the basis that Lord Brennan's ability to advise on this action was limited by the absence of decisive expert input, but Lord Brennan had said that there was no expert input available which would prove causation, without which no case would succeed.

In November 2003, the Legal Services Commission finally decided to withdraw all funding and, in 2004, opposition to this by Alexander Harris Solicitors was withdrawn.

CASES DISMISSED

All campaigning by the Association of Parents ended at that point, both for compensation from the Government and possible compensation through the Courts. Whether other solicitors or other campaign groups will resurrect these issues in the future remains to be seen.

23

The End of the Campaign

It was in August of 1973 that I had first tentatively approached Jack Ashley MP, as he then was, to ask if he would take up the issue of vaccine-damaged children with the then Labour Government. Now, 30 years later, the campaign which we, together with a large number of concerned MPs, had so consistently promoted was suddenly at an end. Along the way, we had lost some of our best helpers and friends, notably Pauline Ashley, who died suddenly in 2003. We last met at the debate in the Lords in June 2000, which saw in the increased payment, and the further meeting we planned never took place, much to my great regret.

The campaign had provided much interest, some discord and a lot of publicity about the principle with which we had been concerned – the requirement that the

Government accepts responsibility for the tragic consequences for the few in their promotion of protection for the many. It had involved the Ombudsman, a Royal Commission and the European Commission of Human Rights in the deliberation of the question of compensation. It had brought together hundreds of families and given them something to fight for on behalf of their damaged children. In the end, it had provided us all with a measure of help with the extra costs which disability creates, which, in most cases, did something to ease the feelings of anger and upset which disability of this kind had caused.

I had grown old with the campaign and was glad to stop. My lovely daughter Helen had settled down in her small home with four other residents and I had come to realise that she was quite happy there. Her accommodation and care were provided by the State and her vaccine-damage payment would ensure that whatever was necessary to take care of all her other wants would be provided. The knowledge that she would be looked after with care and affection when her father and I were no longer alive was comforting, and her two sisters would take over as Trustees to make sure she wanted for nothing.

I am perfectly satisfied with the outcome of the campaign, although aware that for those who hoped for large compensation awards by the Courts, the inability to take legal action was very disappointing. The top-up payment, together with State benefits, provides for the individual. It does not provide money for the benefit of the families, but this was never part of my plan. It is impossible to say if there will ever be another solution to the compensation issue which will satisfy those who wanted family damages as well, but so far there is no evidence that Court action will be possible or that the vaccine manufacturers will feel compelled to award the substantial payment which some families have mentioned, or that the Government will consider making further payments.

Altogether, it took 26 years – from Jack Ashley's first Debate in early 1974 to Alistair Darling's Statement in June 2000 – to get the Government to accept responsibility for the unfortunate damage caused by one of their health programmes. It is possible that, as the years pass, the Government will be asked to increase the £100,000 to take account of inflation, but whether there will ever be another sustained campaign like ours to get a higher level of provision for all remains to be seen and, in all likelihood, I will probably not be around to see it.

Given that any payment from the vaccine manu-facturers would be seen as an admission of liability, opening the floodgates to thousands of claims, it is unlikely that a campaign against them would succeed. What they could do would be to set up a fund to which the family carers of all young disabled people could apply for help with the costs of respite care, holidays, recreational activities and hospital travel. These are costs common to disabilities arising from all sources, whether from vaccine damage, from polio, from the tragic results of rubella in pregnancy, or from the various illness which result in similar tragedies. Such a fund would not only be of immense benefit, but would also do much to enhance the reputations of the manufacturers who, like many other businesses, are seen as being interested only in the profits arising from their sales. It would be wholly appropriate for the vaccine manufacturers to consider such a fund.

Vaccines – Making an
Informed Choice

From the beginning of time, various methods of preventing disease or curing it have been part of folklore. People used plants, drank holy water, talked to witch doctors or practised peculiar rites which they believed would be effective. If people survived a disease, the cure passed into legend and continued, and today there are many people who rely more heavily on homeopathy than on orthodox medicine.

Faced with severe epidemics of serious disease, however, most people turned to their doctors and scientists for answers and relied on vaccination and immunisation to protect them from disease and death.

Until the 1970s, vaccination was a fairly routine affair; routine in the sense that it was accepted as necessary for those faced with possible epidemics of disease without too much concern about or knowledge of possible side-effects. Everyone knew it might hurt, and there are stories of soldiers lining up for injections and fainting before it got to their turn.

Vaccination of babies was, of course, only traumatic for the parent holding the baby, worrying about the pain to be inflicted by the vaccination needle which would make the child cry. This was less upsetting for the parent when the baby was too young to know what was happening; it was more upsetting when the child was a toddler and could see what caused the pain and perhaps blame the parent for letting it happen.

It was only when the campaign for children damaged by vaccination began in the 1970s that mention of risk as well as pain started to be discussed. Parents began to report damage from all vaccines in use since the start of the National Health Service in 1946. A large number said that whooping cough vaccination, given as part of a triple vaccination to their three-month-old babies, had led to severe side-effects which caused brain damage and disability from which there was no recovery. Others blamed smallpox, measles, polio and rubella vaccines for the damage.

Health officials and scientists involved in the promotion of vaccination were not very pleased about mention of vaccine damage and some continue to argue that it was a myth created by parents wanting special provision for their disabled children. There are, of course, convincing arguments in a wealth of published literature to confirm that vaccines, like all medical products, can sometimes cause severe reactions leading to disability. The controversy about vaccine damage springs as much from the determination of health officials on one hand to deny its existence, and anti-vaccinationists on the other to suggest that it results every time someone is vaccinated. Caught in the middle are parents of vaccine-damaged children trying to campaign for their rights.

Some years ago, a German health official, concerned about the moral aspects of vaccination and possible vaccine damage, listed the following as basic requirements for acceptable vaccination programmes: constant research into vaccines in use and methods of improving them; proper education of parents in all aspects of procedures and policies; State acceptance of responsibility for any injuries caused by vaccination policies.

None of these requirements were met in this country until recently, when the Government announced in June 2000 a payment of £100,000 to those damaged by vaccination in the past. When vaccines are suspected of causing damage, withdrawal rather than modification is the preferred option. For instance, following reports of death and injury to children who were vaccinated against measles in 1969, a British Medical report stated that one pharmaceutical company had suspended supply of its measles vaccine. There is no evidence of any published study into the cause of the problem, but at least the withdrawal could be said to have saved other children from potential damage.

There is a stark contrast between the action taken with the measles vaccine and what is happening with the MMR vaccine today. There are many medical experts who question whether MMR is safe. Withdrawing it to carry out research might well provide answers.

Education of parents has always been basic, although there are signs that there have been some improvements recently with more detailed information given in Health Education leaflets available from clinics, with fewer of the upsetting pictures which were part of promotion in the past, like the picture of the very distressed baby gasping and crying on the whooping cough vaccination leaflet, or the picture of a wheelchair with the message 'Sally's mother got rubella and look what Sally got'. This was promotion by fear rather than by intelligent discussion about how the disease could affect babies, or about the likelihood of any particular baby getting the disease in the first place.

Our referral to the Health Service Ombudsman in 1977 resulted in the improvements which have taken place since. The Health Visitor now passes on leaflets to parents or they are displayed at clinics and doctors' surgeries. Some parents have said that once they had received an initial leaflet, they did not get any further information when the vaccination changed or when new ones were added to the schedule. Some leaflets make a brief reference to possible side-effects, but this is generally countered by a statement that damage from the disease is much more serious than any side-effect of the vaccine, and that side-effects would be difficult to prove in any case.

In 1972, for instance, official advice to doctors about whooping cough vaccination was that babies with a history of fits or central nervous system abnormalities should not receive the vaccine. This included cerebral symptoms following asphyxia during birth, and the advice was that where convulsions or any other severe reaction followed triple vaccination, further whooping cough vaccine should not be given.

Advice at the time about measles vaccination was that acute illnesses, or significant sensitivity to hens' eggs, were contraindications and that special consideration was needed before vaccinating children with a history of allergic disease or those with a history or family history of convulsions.

Some of this information became public, but the Department of Health has seldom taken steps to explain why what was considered to be important in the interests of child safety in vaccination 30 years ago is no longer relevant today.

The passage of time and the present policy of rewarding doctors who achieve high acceptance rates by paying them higher fees have resulted in less concentration on possible risk and less discussion of it with the parents concerned.

While it may be difficult to be precise in individual cases, it should nevertheless be possible to give parents as much information as is available about vaccination and disease and help them make a decision based on these facts rather than on worry or fear or pressure from clinics. The attitudes that existed in the past that medical experts knew best and that parents did not need to know too much or would not understand, are no longer acceptable. While many parents will accept whatever advice they are given by doctors and nurses, many others want to be able to discuss the procedure in detail and a lack of opportunity to do so leaves them dissatisfied.

It is clear that the majority of parents want to protect their children and see immunisation as one of the best ways of doing this. There are, of course, a few doctors and parents who regard immunisation as non-effective and dangerous and would advise against it and there are also anti-vaccinationists who paint frightening pictures of what they see as the results of vaccination programmes. The one-sided arguments of anti-vaccinationists cause as much confusion for parents as the one-sided arguments from pro-vaccinationists, and a middle path is necessary.

Vaccination policies are said to be based on a balance of benefits and risks. If only benefits were conferred, there would be no need for secrecy or for discussions about whether to vaccinate or not. But while there are risks, there is an absolute requirement to tell people what these risks are. Secrecy creates suspicion and destroys public confidence, since parents worry as much about what they think is being kept from them as they do about the risks of disease.

VACCINES – MAKING AN INFORMED CHOICE

This section offers some more facts about vaccination for the information of those who might like to do further, more detailed, research. It is not intended to be anti-vaccination, neither is it intended to be an exhaustive survey on the subject. In today's climate, where childhood vaccinations are the subject of much publicity, the following information will provide some interesting insight for those who want to make an informed choice, but have little or no background information and do not know where to go to find it. Much of the detail given about adverse reactions has been copied from official advice.

For those with access to the internet, there are a number of sites giving information. There is a Department of Health site – www.immunisation.nhs.uk – which gives details of the vaccines, the ages at which they should be given, and a lot of other useful information for parents who know nothing about vaccines. Obviously, anything from the Department of Health will be pro-vaccination.

A booklet called *Immunisation against Infectious Disease* is published periodically by the Department of Health, and is available from The Stationery Office (TSO) bookshop for £6.95 (due to have been reprinted in 2005). It also provides a lot of other useful detailed information about vaccines, contraindications, and so on.

There are other websites setting out the arguments against vaccination and parents can become confused reading the pros and cons. A sensible approach is to find out as much as possible about the disease, read the details about who should not be vaccinated, ask about any possible side-effects of the vaccination and then decide. New vaccines will, no doubt, be introduced for diseases which are not causing any concern at present; a vaccination for chicken pox is one which has been mentioned from time to time as a possible addition to the present list. Lots of children get chicken pox without any great concern being expressed by the health officials, but this would change dramatically as soon as a vaccine becomes available and starts to be promoted.

It is worth bearing in mind that immunisation experts can be autocratic and make decisions about your child's health without involving you in the decisions.

IF IN DOUBT, ASK QUESTIONS

If your child is ill after vaccination, don't be put off with the answer that it is probably just a mild upset, that you are being fussy and should just give the child Calpol. Hopefully, it will just be a mild upset, but you need to have your concern treated seriously.

If any illness continues for any length of time after vaccination, keep notes and go back to your doctor. Live virus vaccines can produce illnesses a week or more after vaccination and you need to be sure any illnesses later on are not related to vaccination.

THE BACKGROUND TO VACCINATION POLICIES

Under the National Health Service Act 1946 (variously amended since its inception), it became the duty of the

Health Minister to promote the establishment of a health service designed to secure (among other things) the prevention, diagnosis and treatment of illness 'and for that purpose to provide or secure the effective provision of services'.

Clause 26, Part III of the 1946 Act reads:

(1) Every local health authority shall make arrangements with medical practitioners for the vaccination of persons in the area of the authority against smallpox and the immunisation of such persons against diphtheria.

(2) Any local health authority may, with the approval of the Minister, and if directed by the Minister, make similar arrangements for vaccination or immunisation against any other disease.

(3) In making arrangements under this section, a local health authority shall give every medical practitioner providing general medical services in their area under Part IV of this Act an opportunity to provide services under this section.

(4) The Minister may, either directly or by entering into arrangements with such persons as he thinks fit, supply free of charge to local health authorities and medical practitioners providing services under this section, vaccines, sera or other preparations for vaccinating or immunising persons against any disease.

(5) The Vaccination Acts 1867 to 1907 shall cease to have effect.

In 1946, when the legislation was enacted, smallpox was the disease most prevalent and most feared. Diphtheria was the next potential killer. Concern about whooping cough was beginning to cause concern and 1946 saw the setting up of trials of various vaccines to see which would be beneficial in terms of preventing whooping cough. These trials were interrupted because of the war and were only resumed in 1954.

Under the National Health Service Act, advice to the Minister of Health on the services required or provided by Local Health Authorities was to be given by a Central Health Services Council and, to advise both the Minister and the Central Council, various advisory committees were constituted, their duties being to advise upon such matters relating to the services as they think fit. One such advisory committee is the Joint Committee on Vaccination and Immunisation (JCVI), made up of a number of eminent professors of neurology, microbiology, epidemiology and virology, together with professors from various research and teaching establishments and a few GPs and Health Authority doctors. Doctors from the Department of Health carry out the secretarial functions and the Department also fills the administrative posts.

It is from this Joint Committee that vaccination policies and procedures originate and continue to the present day. From their meetings come the decisions about the introduction of new vaccines or changes in vaccination policies. Surprisingly, although their function is to advise the Minister of Health, they will make public pronouncements and promote vaccination directly when they consider it necessary. The majority are unknown to parents and, concentrated as they are in the fields of research and teaching, the majority have little contact with what goes on in clinics as a result of their decisions.

The Department of Health accepts the recommend-ations of the Joint Committee automatically and passes these down the line to health authorities. There can, however, be occasional upsets in the established routine. On one occasion in 1977, uncertainty about adverse reactions to whooping cough vaccine stemming from parents' reports and research by concerned specialists resulted in the then Secretary of State for Health, David Ennals, refusing to sanction an immunisation promotion campaign designed by the Joint Committee. Interestingly enough, however, this did not stop some members of the Committee going ahead with publicity about the need for vaccination, with warnings of possible disaster from a whooping cough epidemic.

So when the Health Visitor calls on parents to talk to them about vaccination for their babies, she is, in fact, only a small link in the chain of people who have decided what vaccinations are to be given. Having received and accepted the advice of the JCVI, the Department of Health notifies Local Health Authorities about the introduction of a vaccination into its local arrangements.

This is followed by massive media publicity with the message always that the vaccination is necessary to prevent serious diseases which put babies at risk of death or serious injury.

The campaign by the Association of Parents was based on 603 reports of serious reaction to vaccinations. These were as follows:

- Smallpox vaccinations 58 cases
- Polio vaccinations 28 cases
- Measles vaccinations (given singly prior to 1998) 20 cases
- Quad* vaccines 10 cases
- Triple vaccines 487 cases
  (diphtheria, tetanus and whooping cough vaccines, of which whooping cough vaccine was blamed for the damage)

*The quad vaccine was a triple vaccine plus polio vaccine. The use of this vaccine was stopped in the early 1960s.

The 603 reports of vaccine reaction spanned the years 1948 to 1978, which works out at 21 cases of damage per year. During the 30 years, approximately half a million children born each year would be eligible for vaccination. Even assuming that every child was vaccinated and taking what was always the standard line from official medical experts that the chances of vaccine damage are one in a million, this would only have produced 15 cases of severe reaction over the 30 years.

SMALLPOX

Smallpox was the disease which ravaged the world in the eighteenth century and before, and the first attempts to try to protect people against it in this country were made in 1720 when the practice of variolation, which at the time was practised in Turkey, was introduced. The practice involved taking material from smallpox pustules in an infected person and introducing them into an incision made in the arm of the person to be protected. This practice became illegal following the discovery of the Jenner smallpox vaccine which was introduced in the early 1800s and, by 1855, smallpox vaccination was legally compulsory.

Although the vaccination is no longer part of the routine immunisation programme in the UK, it is interesting to look back at some of the events surrounding this policy.

The vaccination apparently proceeded without controversy – or at least any which came to the public notice – from 1855 to around 1920, when a pathologist at a London hospital drew attention to cases of an acute nervous disease of uncertain nature associated with smallpox vaccination and, in 1923, the Minister of Health appointed a special committee – the Andrewes Committee – to carry out an investigation. This investigation was taken over in 1926 by a Committee on Vaccination which reported in 1928 and again in 1930. Over the seven-year period, there had been a total of 183 reported cases of illness affecting the central nervous system, with 94 deaths, which appeared to be associated with vaccination.

The work of both the Andrewes Committee and the Vaccination Committee enabled them to reject the idea that these cases had been caused by coincidental infection from any of the other diseases prevalent at the time.

Some idea of the family tragedies involved can be gleaned from the ages given for those 94 who died: 12 were under a year old, 1 was aged between 2–4 years old, 63 were aged between 5–14 years and 18 were aged over 15 years.

From 1930 onwards, the Ministry of Health continued to collect information about central nervous system illnesses due to smallpox vaccination and, during the next 16 years, to 1946, there was a total of 115 cases of serious illness with 58 deaths, some of these in the Armed Services following recruitment during the war years.

All of this tragedy was occurring at a time when the vaccination was legally compulsory and those who objected could be penalised for failing to have their children vaccinated. Smallpox was still a threat to health and so the official argument against any criticism was that the benefits exceeded the risks. It is doubtful if this excused the attitude of indifference to those who were injured, but the only step taken by the Government was to remove the legal compulsion with the 1946 National Health Service Act. After that, presumably, health officials could argue, as they still do, that since there was no compulsion involved – and by inference this suggested that those who were vaccinated were those who had sought it out and made a free choice – there was no official or other responsibility for those who suffered vaccine damage.

Statistics of vaccine damage continued to be gathered and the next set of figures are perhaps more controversial than those seen previously. Between 1951 and 1970 there were 101 deaths after smallpox vaccination at a time when there were only 47 from smallpox itself. Some of the controversy about this first surfaced publicly in the 1960s when letters to the *Lancet* raised the issue of whether it was right to continue vaccinating in such circumstances. However, the Department of Health had given an assurance to the World Health Organisation that vaccination would continue in this country in support of the world smallpox eradication programme. In the event, the vaccination was withdrawn here in 1972 to criticism from countries who kept it as part of their routine programme. It is not clear whether any attempt was made by the Department of Health to investigate the condition of those children to whom vaccination had been offered as protection and who had suffered severe damage as a result, but certainly their moral obligation to compensate them for their injuries was never considered.

The Department of Health now states that 'there is no indication for smallpox vaccination for any individual, with the exception of some laboratory staff and specific workers at identifiable risk,' and adds that 'advice on the need for vaccination and contraindications can be obtained from the Public Health Laboratory Service Virus Reference Laboratory'.

58 reports of damage from smallpox vaccination which had occurred between 1948 and 1972 were included in the Association's total list. These were young adults still living with their disabilities. We had no reports from families where children had died and it is not known if the cause of death in these cases was known to the public.

MEASLES

The 20 cases of reaction to measles vaccination reported to the Association were from 1968 onwards when measles vaccination was given singly at the age of 15 months. This was long before the introduction of the MMR (measles, mumps and rubella) vaccination.

Trials of measles vaccines had been carried out for some years before the vaccination was introduced as a safe method of preventing the disease. One of these trials was held in 1965 in a small residential nursery in the south of England with a vaccine developed by Burroughs Wellcome called Welcovax. The doctors and others involved in the trial went to some lengths to check for reactions, carrying out EEG readings on the vaccinees on various days after vaccination and noting the mild but definite clinical changes which occurred and the rash which occurred in some cases.

Despite this, the vaccine was developed and was used in the measles vaccination programme which began in 1968. Early in 1969 however, Burroughs Wellcome issued a statement following withdrawal of the vaccine 'because of recent reports of a few isolated cases of complications involving the central nervous system which arose in children within about eight days of the vaccination'. Encephalitis was recorded as a complication for some children and the British Medical Association, while praising the manufacturers for their prompt action in withdrawing the vaccine, promised to take all steps possible to inform family doctors.

Presumably, there is a report somewhere of a study to decide what went wrong and why the vaccine was allowed to be issued in the first place, bearing in mind the details of the 1965 trials in the nursery in the South. If such a report exists it was never published for the information of the public.

The measles vaccination programme continued in 1969 with another measles vaccine but there is some evidence to suggest that doctors informed about the Welcovax vaccine were less than happy with the vaccination programme. Some did not promote it very strongly and, even today, there are a few doctors who will say that good medical care for any child getting measles would be a better option than measles vaccination.

A Study set up in 1976 (the National Childhood Encephalopathy Study [NCES]) to look at reactions to whooping cough vaccine also studied reactions to measles vaccination and reported that, while 1 in 100,000 children were affected by whooping cough vaccine, the figure for measles vaccine was higher at 1 in 87,000.

Single measles vaccine has now been replaced by the MMR vaccine and the Department of Health says the vaccine used is an attenuated virus vaccine which is not transmitted and vaccinated persons cannot pass on infection.

Adverse Reactions

Most of the reactions reported referred to a very high fever eight days after vaccination leading to encephalitis; severe convulsions which continued and caused brain damage; or a bad measles rash with caused illness and discomfort, in some cases leading to the disease itself.

THE TRIPLE AND THE FIVE-IN-ONE

The triple is the name which most parents recognise as meaning diphtheria, tetanus and whooping cough vaccination. There are at least a few parents who only know the name but don't know what it contains – an illustration, perhaps, of how routine immunisation has become over the years.

The name no longer exists since the introduction of the 'Five-in-One' in September 2004, which contains the same three vaccines – diphtheria, tetanus and whooping cough, and the added polio and haemophilus influenzae type B (Hib).

1. Diphtheria Vaccination

Research on tetanus and diphtheria antitoxins was carried out in the early 1890s, but a satisfactory diphtheria vaccine was only available in this country during the 1930s following vaccine trials. Between 1941 and 1943, a mass vaccination campaign was carried out with the intention of vaccinating children up to the age of 15 years, and this was credited by health officials as having rapidly decreased the incidence of diphtheria.

Notices appeared all over the country in the 1940s saying 'DIPHTHERIA IS DEADLY – BE IMMUNISED', and the campaign was credited by health officials as having rapidly decreased the incidence of diphtheria.

Today, very few cases of diphtheria occur and health officials say that most of the cases which do occur are imported. Between 1979 and 1988, 31 cases of diphtheria were reported, with only 1 death.

Critics say that this means there is no further need to keep vaccinating small children. Health officials point out that in view of the small number of cases of the disease, there is no opportunity for children to acquire a natural immunity and vaccination must continue.

Adverse Reactions

There can be swelling at injection site, some temporary fever or headache. Very rare reactions are said to be anaphylactic shock or neurological reactions.

Children suffering from any acute illness should not be vaccinated until better. Reactions to a preceding dose means vaccination should not proceed further.

Only one case of reaction to diphtheria vaccination given singly was reported to the Association during the years of the campaign.

2. Anti-Tetanus Vaccination

Reports about the production of tetanus toxoid first appeared in the 1890s and it was widely used in the British Army in the First and Second World Wars. It was subsequently combined with diphtheria toxoid to form the 'double vaccine' which was used in the mid-1950s before whooping cough vaccine was added to form the triple. This double vaccine was, until recently, available for parents who, for any reason, did not wish their children to have whooping cough vaccine but, with the advent of the Five-in-One, this arrangement no longer exists.

Anti-tetanus vaccine is also available separately for adults, such as those working on the land who may be at risk from tetanus, the spores of which are present in the soil. For adults and children over ten years of age, the recommended schedule is vaccination at ten-year intervals. The Department of Health has said that more frequent vaccinations are not necessary and can cause considerable local reactions.

Adverse Reactions

Swelling and redness at injection site. Headache and fever may occur. A small nodule may appear at the injection site but it generally disappears without problems. There are occasional reports of neurological problems following the vaccination, mostly among adults who may have been vaccinated too frequently.

A child who has a severe reaction to a preceding dose should not be given further vaccination. Where a child is suffering a serious illness, vaccination should wait until the child is fully better.

Only two of all the reports to the Association mentioned a reaction to tetanus vaccination.

3. Whooping Cough (Pertussis) Vaccine

This vaccine was officially introduced in 1957, following trials of the vaccine which had been taking place since 1940. The trials were carried out in cities all over the country and were intended to find out which of the vaccines then available were the best. Some vaccines were imported from America and some were manufactured in the UK and, by 1957, health officials were convinced that they were then able to recommend the UK vaccines which, they said, appeared to give a high degree of protection against the disease.

In 1967, ten years after the introduction of the vaccination programme, reports by medical experts (particularly, that by Professor George Dick) suggested that the vaccine appeared to be causing a high rate of serious reaction and brain damage. Shortly afterwards, the Public Health Laboratory Service said that the vaccine did not appear to be very effective. Many vaccinated children were getting whooping cough and passing it on to their baby siblings. At the time, the recommended age for first vaccination was three months.

Following these reports, the Department of Health increased the strength of the vaccine to make it more effective. The reports about the dangers of the vaccine appear to have gone unheeded, apart, perhaps, from a strong defence of the vaccine by one of its manufacturers and attempts to belittle the evidence produced by Professor Dick. As always, health officials and vaccine manufacturers concentrated all their efforts on protecting the vaccine and showed no concern for any damaged children who may have suffered from it. The only concession made to concerns expressed about possible damage was changing the age at which the new vaccine was given to six months instead of three.

When the Association of Parents was set up in 1973 to campaign about vaccine damage, the vast majority of reports from parents blamed whooping cough vaccination for damage to their children. At the time, there was no public knowledge of the concerns expressed six years previously by Professor Dick, a member of the Joint Committee on Vaccination and Immunisation, and these only came to light when the large volume of letters accusing whooping cough vaccine of having caused serious injury prompted some research.

So well had the concerns expressed in 1967 been rebutted by the health officials and manufacturers that there was little knowledge among parents and doctors of what was happening.

Today, 37 years later, whooping cough vaccine is still promoted and doctors generally state that it is a new vaccine, and not the same as the one which 'caused the scare'. The present vaccine is described as 'a suspension of killed bordetella pertussis'. In 1996, a new 'acellular' whooping cough vaccine was made available and it was said to be safer, but not as effective, as the vaccine in use.

Adverse Reactions

Reactions considered to be acceptable are swelling and redness at the site of vaccination and the appearance of a small, painless nodule which usually disappears.

More serious reactions are prolonged unusual screaming, collapse, convulsions, fever of 39.5°C or over, prolonged unresponsiveness, a large, very hard, red and swollen area spread over most of the thigh or arm where the vaccination was administered.

If any of the above serious reactions occur, further vaccinations should not be given.

The Department of Health now says that conditions such as asthma, eczema, convulsions in the family, prematurity, cerebral palsy and Downs Syndrome are not contraindications to vaccination, although these have been listed as contraindications in the past.

Perhaps one of the problems concerning contraindications is the fact that vaccinations now start at the age of two months. At that age, babies spend a lot of time sleeping and they have only just begun to focus and smile, and show an awareness of their surroundings. It would be difficult to determine whether there was any predisposition to conditions such as severe eczema, infantile spasms or convulsions, or any other condition which might have a bearing on their suitability for vaccinations.

It is a fact that the schedule of vaccinations has been arranged so that most vaccinations can be given with the minimum of trips to the clinic and at the earliest age. It is generally accepted that parents are not as worried about babies crying as they are about the cries of distressed older infants and toddlers who will be more aware of what is happening to them.

There has been very little discussion about the safest – as opposed to the most convenient – age to vaccinate babies. One study group in Oxford, however, has expressed the view that, since maternal antibodies protect babies up to the age of about six months, it would be reasonable to suggest that vaccination is not effective, and therefore should not commence, before that age. The Department of Health, on the other hand, says that maternal antibodies are no longer an issue after the age of two months.

The vast majority of reports to the Association referred to whooping cough vaccination and it was on this vaccine and the damage it had caused that the Association based its campaign to the Government to accept some responsibility for the damaged children involved.

Of the total of 600 cases of damage referred, 487 referred to whooping cough vaccine, more than four times the total of all the other cases combined. In most cases, the reaction was an exceptionally high fever, followed by convulsions from which the child never recovered, and most of the vaccine-damaged children in this group are brain damaged, have continuing epilepsy, either have little speech or do not speak at all and cannot live any kind of normal life; some are physically disabled as well, and all need 24-hour care and attention.

The Government eventually accepted responsibility for these young adults and paid £100,000 to each to make provision to secure extra care for them, despite which some official health cynics continue to argue that whooping cough vaccine damage was all 'a scare'.

4. Haemophilus Influenzae Type B (Hib)

This vaccination was introduced in 1992 to protect children against haemophilus influenza type B, a disease which can cause meningitis, epiglottis (causing breathing difficulties, croup), blood poisoning, pneumonia, septic arthritis and heart disease. Because meningitis is the most common result of the disease, the vaccination has become known among parents as a vaccination against meningitis.

The disease occurs from the age of three months, reaching a peak at about a year and then declining to four years of age after which infection is uncommon.

Official statistics suggest that the incidence of cases in England and Wales rose from 869 in 1983 to 1,259 in 1989 – which led to the decision to vaccinate.

The vaccine is, in layman's terms, a 'manufactured' vaccine – neither a live virus or dead vaccine but a combination of bacterial antigens.

Adverse Reactions

There can be swelling and redness at the injection site following the first dose. This is said to occur three to four hours after vaccination and should disappear within 24 hours.

Acute illness means the vaccination should be postponed. A severe local reaction means immunisation should not proceed.

5. Polio Vaccine

Routine vaccination against polio began in the UK in the mid 1950s using Salk vaccine imported from America. Although this was a killed virus vaccine, there were some worries about its use because of an incident in America following the use of the vaccine when a large number of people developed polio from one batch. However, the UK authorities considered it a risk worth taking in view of the dangers of the disease itself. Salk vaccine was then manufactured in the UK and used until 1962, when a new live virus vaccine known as Sabin vaccine was introduced. This vaccine has continued in use until the present day.

There was also concern about the use of a live virus polio vaccine when it began because of the possibility of causing poliomyelitis in vaccinated persons or their contacts and the Public Health Laboratory Service took responsibility for setting up surveillance schemes which started in 1962 and continue to the present day. These are designed to record cases where the vaccination produces the disease, so that the experts can keep a check on the balance of benefits against risks. They do, however, keep the information to themselves and it was not until the late 1970s that a Department of Health leaflet for parents mentioned the possibility of a child or the child's parents developing polio after vaccination. The polio virus can be found in the faeces and, considering the strict advice which should have been given to parents about the handling and disposal of nappies, but was not mentioned, it is perhaps surprising that the number of vaccine polio cases was not much higher than was recorded.

Adverse Reactions

Live virus oral polio vaccine can cause polio in the vaccinated baby or person, and also in contacts of the vaccinated baby or person. These cases are now more noticeable because polio from the natural wild virus has been eliminated in the UK and all cases of polio occurring since 1985 (approximately 20, of which 3 were imported and 4 were contact cases) have resulted from the vaccine. To try to avoid contact cases (where the virus is passed from the vaccinated baby to the adult parent or carer) the Department of Health now stresses the need for strict personal hygiene – particularly after handling nappies.

Vaccination should be postponed if the child has an acute or feverish illness, has vomiting or diarrhoea, is receiving corticosteroids or similar treatment, or suffers a malignant condition which impairs the immune system.

Vaccination should not be given during pregnancy – the Department says during the first four months of pregnancy, but many women worry about being vaccinated at any stage during pregnancy in case of damage to the foetus.

Where it is known that a child is immunosuppressed (cannot produce antibodies against infectious disease), oral polio vaccine should not be introduced into the house by way of vaccination of other members of the family.

The World Health Organisation (WHO) has declared the UK a polio-free zone, but has asked the Health Department to continue with the vaccination programme until the last reported case of polio has been eradicated globally. The WHO says that stopping the vaccination too soon could lead to a resurgence of the disease and points to what happened in the Netherlands when 68 cases of polio were confirmed in February 1993, with 2 deaths, and it is suggested that the outbreaks occurred among religious groups opposed to immunisation.

It is the aim of the World Health Organisation to encourage the continuance of the vaccination until the disease is wiped out, not only with public health in mind but also with the idea of saving the vast costs associated with the prevention and treatment of the disease – a saving which the WHO estimates would be US$3 billion by the year 2015.

When a disease is wiped out, the side-effects of continuing vaccination can more clearly be demonstrated. For instance, there has been no case of 'natural' polio in the UK since 1987, but there have been at least 13 cases of polio from the vaccine.

The number of cases of damage following polio vaccination referred to the Association was 28.

MENINGITIS C

This was introduced in the mid-1990s to be given with the other primary vaccinations. It is also given to all children up to the age of 18. It does not protect against meningitis B, which accounts for most of the reported cases. The vaccine is given at the same time as the first of the Five-in-One vaccinations, but in a different site.

Immunisations in the Five-in-One programme are given to babies at two, three and four months, with a further combined immunisation at between three and five years – before school entry.

MEASLES, MUMPS AND RUBELLA (MMR)

This vaccination was introduced in the UK in 1988. Before that, there was no routine vaccination in England and Wales for mumps; rubella vaccination was given to girls only at around age 13 (and to mothers found after the birth of a baby to have no immunity to rubella) and measles vaccination was given as a single vaccination at around 15 months.

Introduction of the MMR vaccination changed the rubella immunisation policy from one which was designed to offer individual protection to girls 'approaching child-bearing age' and non-immune mothers, to a policy of eliminating the disease by vaccinating babies of both sexes. It also overcame the medical concern about a poor uptake for measles vaccination as it was felt that by adding measles to what was to be called another 'triple' (a name familiar to parents), a higher acceptance rate would be achieved which proved to be the case initially. In the promotion of the third component of the vaccine – mumps vaccine – reference was made to the various complications which could arise from the disease, including meningitis and other neurological complications.

At the time of the introduction of the vaccination in 1988, the possible adverse reactions as listed by the Department of Health were malaise, fever and/or a rash, which might occur about a week afer vaccination and last two to three days, febrile convulsions during the sixth to eleventh days after vaccination, glandular swelling in the third week after vaccination, mumps meningitis occasionally and thrombocytopenia.

In addition to the above, medical research carried out after the launch of the vaccination suggested that the live virus mumps vaccine could cause neurosensory problems – i.e. affecting sight, hearing and balance. Research carried out in the Manchester area suggested that vaccinated children were suffering a higher proportion of joint pains and arthritic conditions than were present in the general community, conditions which can result from rubella vaccination.

In September 1992, the Department of Health decided to withdraw vaccines manufactured by two manu-facturers – Pluserix-MMR, manufactured by Smith Kline and French, and Immravax, manufactured by Merieux – leaving the MMR 11 vaccine manufactured by Wellcome as the only one in use. The reason for this, according to the Department, was that the two withdrawn vaccines were found to have a higher risk of causing mumps meningitis – the risk with the Wellcome vaccine being 'lower'. The Department said that the meningitis caused by the vaccines was transient, suggesting that children recovered from the illness without any serious effects.

The withdrawal of the two vaccines caused a lot of publicity, following which a few parents began to report illnesses in their children following MMR vaccination and publicity about cases of meningitis which had resulted from the vaccination increased public concern.

Then came the mass MR (measles and rubella) vaccination of eight million UK schoolchildren in 1994 with reports of more than 2,700 adverse reactions, affecting 1,202 children. The Department of Health produced an analysis of all the reactions, concluding that the majority were minor and, where reports of serious reactions were concerned, the Department concluded that the reports did not necessarily imply a causal relationship and that, in some cases, the reactions would be coincidental. As far as the Department was concerned, there was nothing to worry about, but parents worrying about their sick children felt differently.

Parents then heard about the study Dr Andrew Wakefield was carrying out at the Royal Free Hospital into inflammatory bowel disease with a link to autism, and those who felt that the inflammatory bowel disease their children were suffering had resulted from their MMR vaccination, sought his help for treatment of their childrens' condition. There was then widespread publicity about bowel disease, autism and MMR vaccination and large numbers of parents approached solicitors to investigate the possibility of legal action.

More than 2,000 families were joined in this campaign which was organised by the JABS group who worked long and hard to help the parents concerned. Whereas legal aid was first given to the solicitors to help investigate the cases, this funding has now been withdrawn and is unlikely to be given again unless and until scientists can demonstrate causation, which is a prerequisite of court action in any vaccine-damage case. Whereas claims under the Government payment scheme are dealt with 'on the balance of probabilities', the Courts require scientific proof of the exact chain of events from the giving of the vaccine to the creation of the damage, something which no scientist has so far been able to demonstrate.

There have been calls from parents to have the measles vaccine administered separately while they decide about mumps and rubella, about which many are less concerned. However, the Department of Health has rejected this on the grounds that any delay between the vaccinations could leave children at risk of mumps and rubella, and have not agreed to separate measles vaccine. Very few parents would be aware of the past history of single measles vaccine, but the Department of Health is, and that may form some part of their reluctance to return to single vaccines.

One drawback of their decision could be that girls not now receiving rubella vaccine because of parental refusal of MMR might well be at risk of rubella when they reach 'child-bearing age', which could have disastrous consequences.

Adverse Reactions

Vaccination should be postponed if a child is suffering from an acute illness. It should not be carried out in children suffering from any malignant disease; those who have received another live vaccine within three weeks; those with allergies to neomycin or kanamycin; within three months of an injection of immunoglobulin. Allergy to eggs is no longer considered important.

TUBERCULOSIS (BCG)

Although this is not part of routine childhood immunisations, a number of enquiries have been received from parents who have been offered BCG vaccination for babies. The official DoH policy is intended to cover the vaccination of:

- School children between the ages of 10 and 13 years
- Students, including those in teacher-training colleges
- Newborn babies, children or adults – *where the parents or individuals themselves request the BCG vaccination*

The last sentence is significant – the guidelines specify the aspect of individual requests. Some parents who have not

275

requested the vaccination for their newborn babies say they have been pressed to have this without any explanation.

The above groups are said to be 'at normal risk' of the disease. There are other groups said to be at higher risk of contracting the disease and these are mainly health service staff, veterinary staff, close contacts of persons suffering from TB, immigrants from countries at higher risk and those intending to go to countries where TB is prevalent.

Before vaccination is given, a tuberculin skin test is carried out on all except newborn babies, who, the Department says, do not need the test. This test can have a positive result – i.e. which indicates that the person has been successfully immunised, or has been infected in the past. A negative result indicates the need for immunisation.

TB vaccination should not take place where there has been any previous severe local or general reaction to immunisation; receiving steroid treatment; suffering from malignant conditions (e.g. leukaemia); with faulty immune systems; anyone sensitive to TB protein; suffering from a fever; or for those with septic skin conditions.

Following immunisation, the arm used for the BCG immunisation should not be used for further injections for a few months.

Adverse Reactions

A local reaction is expected at the immunisation site between two to six weeks. This is a small pimple which widens into a small circular area with some crusting. Sometimes, the area can become ulcerous and a scab will develop.

A severe adverse reaction is when the reaction site described above develops a large ulcer and abscess. Records exist of a number of such cases, where plastic surgery was eventually required on the arm used for the injection. According to the Department of Health, this can happen if incorrect injection technique is used and there are strict rules governing the method of injection and the injection site.

Occasionally, the injected organisms can travel through the body, affecting lungs and causing the disease. Anaphylactic reactions – i.e. severe allergic shock reactions which can cause collapse and sometimes death – are also possible.

Up to the 1980s, TB was declining in this country to such an extent that medical experts were beginning to argue against the policy of vaccinating large numbers of children, and causing some scarring of arms in the process, in order to save a small number of cases of the disease each year. At one stage, there was such a shortage of vaccine – possibly because manufacturers thought the vaccination policy might be cancelled – that vaccinations were delayed in some areas.

In recent years, it is said that there has been an increase in the incidence of the disease, with over 5,000 new cases being reported each year, and this has been said to have resulted from high immigration from areas where the disease exists.

Only two or three cases of damage following BCG vaccination have been reported to the Association.

INFLUENZA

Again, this vaccination is not part of the programme of routine immunisation of children, although some details are included in view of some reports from parents that the vaccination has been given to their babies and young children as if it was part of the routine programme, without any discussion or explanation.

Influenza vaccines are prepared each year using the virus strains considered to be the most likely ones to circulate. However, it is readily admitted by health experts that since they cannot always foretell what strains will be circulating, it can only be hoped that the vaccine available will lessen the severity of the disease.

The prepared vaccines are about 70 per cent effective, which means vaccinated persons can still get influenza, and the protection lasts about 12 months, which means annual vaccinations are necessary.

The vaccination is specially aimed at those at most risk of complications from influenza and the categories are listed as: those with respiratory disease, including asthma; with heart disease; suffering renal failure; with diabetes; with immunity problems resulting from disease or treatment of disease; residents of nursing homes, old people's homes and other long-stay facilities.

Immunisation of fit children and adults is not routinely recommended.

Adverse Reactions

There can be soreness at the immunisation site. Fever, malaise and myalgia 6–12 hours after immunisation, lasting up to 2 days, is possible. Rash, glandular swelling, bronchospasm and anaphylactic shock reactions can occur.

Severe sensitivity to hens' eggs contraindicates this vaccination. Pregnancy is also a contraindication.

Death following influenza vaccination has been reported occasionally in the press. Details are seldom given of the outcome of post mortem and the final diagnosis of the cause of death, and it is therefore always difficult to say with certainty whether the vaccination caused the fatality. However, since it is known that anaphylactic shock – which is listed as a reaction to the vaccination – can result in death, it is reasonable to assume that the vaccination occasionally results in death.

THE VACCINE DAMAGE PAYMENT SCHEME

The Payment Scheme was set up in 1978 to pay £10,000 to anyone severely damaged by any of the vaccinations promoted by the Department of Health. All of the letters and claims received by the Association of Parents were passed on to the Vaccine Damage Payment Unit who then set up a system of examining claims 'on the balance of probabilities'.

The Payment Scheme became The Vaccine Damage Payment Act 1979. There were periodic increases in the payment, the payment in 1999 being £14,000. Up to

1996, the total of applications to the Payment Unit was 3,667, of which 876 claims were successful.

In June 2000, the Government increased the payment to £100,000, following which further claims were made by parents who considered that vaccination had injured their children.

Assessing the 'balance of probabilities' requires certain details and records to be available in support of claims. For example, the probable cause of damage would be the reaction to immmunisation if details are available to show that:

- the child was born normally and was reported to be perfectly healthy at birth
- there was healthy development to the date of vaccination, without any illness which might cause damage
- there is a record of the vaccination in question, together with a record of a noticeable reaction to the vaccination, with details of the exact interval between vaccination and reaction, and this was reported to the doctor
- despite medical investigations and treatment, no cause for the child's condition was found, other than the reaction to vaccination

If, on the other hand, medical checks showed other conditions in the child which could cause damage, then there would be a balance of probabilities and doctors would decide which was the most likely cause.

Claim forms for vaccine damage are available from:

The Vaccine Damage Payments Unit
Palatine House
Lancaster Road
Preston PR1 1HB

Payments are made for damage amounting to 60 per cent disability. In the case of physical disability, this is judged according to the Industrial Injuries Scheme where percentages are quoted for various physical disabilities. There has never been any clear definition of what 60 per cent is in the case of someone who is mentally disabled, but the rules which apply to disability benefits in general, such as the need for constant attendance, or help with mobility, cover it.

The initial claim is checked in the Payment Unit; doctors and specialists who have been involved in the care and treatment of the disabled person are generally asked for reports which form part of the Unit's examination of the claim. If the claim is refused, the claimant has a right of appeal to a tribunal, made up of a lawyer and two medical experts with knowledge of vaccine damage.

When a claimant asks for an appeal hearing, the payment unit sends on copies of all medical reports received, so that the claimant has an opportunity to ensure all relevant facts are included.

If the appeal fails, there is a right of a further appeal if it can be shown that the tribunal made a mistake as to some fact or overlooked some vital piece of medical evidence. Otherwise, the decision is final.

For a successful claim, a sum of £100,000 is paid under a Deed of Trust to the parents or Trustees of the disabled person. It is paid as a 'discretionary' Trust which gives the Trustees authority to use the money for the benefit of the disabled person and to invest it in various ways. The payment does not affect the benefits already being received and does not have to be used to pay for residential care.

There have been incidents where local DSS offices paying benefits to vaccine-damaged children have queried the use of the payment and initially reduced the benefits. The Vaccine Damage Payment Unit has produced leaflets to correct this.

The Association of Parents of Vaccine Damaged Children can be contacted on:
Tel: 01608 661595
Fax: 01608 663432
E-mail: rosemary277@btinternet.com

Reference Sources and Articles

The authors, titles and reports listed below have formed some of the valuable research material for this book, and provide a wealth of information for those who wish to become better informed, and so take control of those important decisions that sometimes turn out to be life-changing.

British Medical Journal (1960). Bower BD and Jeavons PM

Neurological complications of pertussis inoculation. Archives of Disease in Childhood 49: 46-49 (1974). Kuhlenkampff M, Schwartzman JS, Wilson J

Reports by Globus and Kohn (1949); Toomey (1949): Anderson and Morris (1950); Kong (1953); Thursby,

Pelham and Giles (1958); Strom (1960)

References to some of the Expert Research Which
Helped me to Prepare My Case

Neurological Sequelae of Prophylactic Inoculation
Henry G Miller and John B Stanton.
(Quarterly Journal of Medicine = New Series xx111
No 89 January 1954)
(A review of the literature on the subject of neurological
complications)

Neurological Complications of Pertussis Immunization
J M Berg MB Bch Msc
British Medical Journal July 5 1958
A listing of 25 Medical Authors who reported serious
reactions

Reactions to Combined Vaccines containing killed
Bordetella Pertussis
Margaret Haire MD Belfast; D S Dane BA MB Cantab
MRCP MC Path.
George Dick MD DscEdin, FRCP Lond FRCP Edin,
FCPath.
Reporting studies to determine the nature of serious
reactions.

Immunisation Against Whooping Cough
A B Christie MA MD DPH DCH

REFERENCE SOURCES AND ARTICLES
A report on the preparation testing, etc of Pertussis
vaccines

Reactions to Routine Immunisations in Childhood
Professor George Dick Proceedings of the Royal Society
of Medicine Vol 67 May 1974

Archives of Disease in Childhood 1974
Kulenkampff L et al
Reporting study of 36 children with a neurological
disorder following triple vaccine, carried out by Dr John
Wilson at Great Ormond Street Hospital

Vaccination against Whooping Cough: Efficacy verus Risks
Gordon T Stewart University of Glasgow.   The Lancet
January 29 1977

*Pertuss Immunisation and Serious Acute Neurological Illnesses
in Children*
David Miller, Nicola Madge, Judith Diamond,
Jane Wadsworth, Euan Ross
A study to determine the long term outcome of serious
neurological illness associated with pertussis immunisation
B M J volume 307 6 November 1993

Surveillance of Salk Vaccination in England and Wales 1956-61
Dr A T Rode, Ministry of Health Proceedings of Royal
Society of Medicine 464 1964

HELEN'S STORY

Inoculation and Poliomyelitis
British Medical Journal July 1, 1950 A Bradford Hill
Dsc PhD and J Knowelden MD DPH

*The Relation of Prophylactic Inoculations to the Onset
of Poliomyelitis* – Bertram P Mccloskey MB Melb
The Lancet April 8th 1950
*Illnesses attributed to Smallpox Vaccination during 1951
to 1960*